13-Week Devotional

Moses and Jesus and Me!

Discovering Jesus in the Old Testament Stories of Moses

FOR BOYS AGES 10–12

Moses and Jesus and Me!

Copyright © 2019 Rose Publishing, LLC.

RoseKidz® is an imprint of
Rose Publishing, LLC
P.O. Box 3473
Peabody, Massachusetts 01961-3473
www.hendricksonrose.com/rosekidz
All rights reserved.

Cover design by Emily Heintz
Interior design by Drew McCall

No part of this book may be reproduced or transmitted in any form or by any means, electronic or mechanical, including photocopying, recording, or by any information storage and retrieval system, without permission in writing from the publisher.

Unless otherwise indicated, all Scripture quotations are taken from the Holy Bible, New Living Translation, copyright © 1996, 2004, 2015 by Tyndale House Foundation. Used by permission of Tyndale House Publishers, Inc., Carol Stream, Illinois 60188. All rights reserved.

Scripture quotations marked (NIrV) are taken from the Holy Bible, New International Reader's Version®, NIrV ® Copyright © 1995, 1996, 1998, 2014 by Biblica, Inc.™ Used by permission of Zondervan. All rights reserved worldwide. www.zondervan.com The "NIrV" and "New International Reader's Version" are trademarks registered in the United States Patent and Trademark Office by Biblica, Inc.™

ISBN: 978-1-62862-831-9
RoseKidz Reorder #L50038
JUVENILE NONFICTION/Religious/Christian/Devotional & Prayer

Printed in the United States of America
Printed in July 2019

Contents

Introduction: The Backstory 5

Activity Supply List 7

Week 1: Planned by God
  Great Plans 10
  Looking for Jesus 18

Week 2: Protected by God
  Astonishing Protection 26
  Learning to Rest 34

Week 3: Called by God
  The Perfect Job 42
  Selfie Service 50

Week 4: Made Strong by God
  Power and Authority 58
  Growing Confident 66

Week 5: Encouraged by God
  Courage in Chaos 74
  Facing Fears 82

Week 6: Saved by God
  First and Last 90
  Giving My All 98

Week 7: Freed by God
- True Freedom 106
- Living in Freedom 114

Week 8: Helped by God
- God Does the Impossible 122
- Asking Always 130

Week 9: Led by God
- God Guides 138
- Listen and Obey 146

Week 10: Asking God
- God Provides 154
- Trusting Completely 162

Week 11: Loving God
- Perfect Commands 172
- Living by Jesus' Law 180

Week 12: Confessing to God
- Forgetting Who You Are 188
- What Is Forgiveness? 196

Week 13: Sticking with God
- Promised Land 204
- Growing in Faithfulness 212

Answer Key 220

Introduction

The Backstory

If you've read the Bible or been to church, then you probably know some things about Moses and Jesus. Moses lived great adventures and freed millions of people from slavery. Jesus preached to thousands and died for our sins. Let's recap Moses' and Jesus' story so that we're all reminded of God's greatness.

For nearly 400 years, the Israelites lived in Egypt. The Pharaoh was afraid that they would rebel against him so he forced them into slavery. He thought this would make them weaker, but the Israelites continued to grow. Pharaoh ordered his guards to throw all the baby Israelite boys into the Nile river. It was a scary time for the Israelites. But one mother hid her baby in a waterproof basket.

She prayed for God to protect her son and she pushed the basket into the Nile River. God answered her prayer. The princess of Egypt found the baby and named him Moses. She raised him as her own son at Pharaoh's palace. Eventually, Moses lead God's people to freedom.

Moses was an amazing hero.

- He was a prophet who spoke God's words.
- He was a savior who freed millions of people.
- He talked with God face-to-face.

But God promised Moses that another prophet was coming who would be even greater than Moses. God said, "I will raise up a prophet like you [Moses] from among their fellow Israelites. I will put my words in his mouth, and he will tell the people everything I command him" (Deuteronomy 18:18).

God's Law (given through Moses) was the center of everything the Israelites did. So, they were looking for a Messiah like Moses. In Jesus' day, the Israelites expected the Messiah to free them from the hated Romans. They didn't yet know that Jesus was greater than Moses. They didn't understand that Jesus was doing something far bigger than everything Moses did! "Jesus deserves far more glory than Moses, just as a person who builds a house deserves more praise than the house itself" (Hebrews 3:3).

We're going to look at ways that Moses' story and Jesus' story are alike. But then, we're going to study the amazing ways Jesus is far greater—and how these truths can change your life!

Activity Supply List

Many activities in this devotional require supplies. Some are reoccurring and are listed under the Basic Craft Materials list or the Basic Kitchen Materials list. These should be on hand at all times. Other materials are listed under the "additional materials" lists for specific weeks. Consider looking ahead a week or two so that you are prepared for the activities as they arise.

Basic Craft Materials

- ruler
- scissors
- white glue
- tape
- colored paper
- white paper
- black paper
- permanent markers
- markers
- pencils
- index cards
- butcher paper

Basic Kitchen Materials

- plastic wrap
- mixing bowl
- large spoon
- silverware
- measuring spoons
- water
- ice
- sugar
- salt
- vanilla extract
- baking sheet

Additional Materials for Week 1

- heavy paper
- Post-it Notes in three colors (optional)

Additional Materials for Week 2

- small sheets of poster board (9x12 inch) (or a ring-bound sketch pad)
- hole punch
- binder ring
- watercolors
- paintbrushes
- cookie sheet and tray
- table salt
- eyedropper (optional)
- food coloring (optional)
- marshmallows
- stick of butter
- cinnamon
- crescent roll dough

Additional Materials for Week 4

- wipes
- magnifying glass

Additional Materials for Week 5

- gallon- and quart-sized resealable freezer bags
- half-and-half
- rock salt or ice-cream salt
- smooth rocks
- gloves or hand towel (optional)
- acrylic paints and paintbrushes (optional)

Additional Materials for Week 6

- apple
- raisins or dates
- walnuts
- cinnamon
- honey
- grape juice
- blender
- clear glass
- red food coloring
- bleach
- basketball

Additional Materials for Week 10

- food coloring
- clear plastic tubing, quarter inch
- can or length or
- wide PVC pipe
- clear packing tape
- posterboard (optional)
- paper fastener (optional)

Additional Materials for Week 11

- copy of 10 Commandments
- newspaper
- poster board or heavy paper
- masking tape or sticky tack

Additional Materials for Week 12

- clear Con-Tact paper (optional)

Additional Materials for Week 13

- latex or rubber gloves
- trash bags
- watercolor paper and paint
- paintbrushes
- (optional) recycled materials (egg carton, soda bottle, soup can, etc.)

Week 1 • Day 1

Planned by God

Long ago God spoke many times and in many ways to our ancestors through the prophets. And now in these final days, he has spoken to us through his Son. God promised everything to the Son as an inheritance, and through the Son he created the universe.

HEBREWS 1:1-2

"For I know the plans I have for you," says the Lord. "They are plans for good and not for disaster, to give you a future and a hope."

JEREMIAH 29:11

Great Plans

EXODUS 1:1-2:10; MATTHEW 1:18-25; HEBREWS 1

Surprising Similarities

Here are some surprising similarities between Jesus and Moses:

Born into **Gentile** Empires

- Moses was born in the Egyptian Empire.
- Jesus was born in Israel, but it was controlled by the Roman Empire.

> **Gentile**
> any person who is not Jewish

Born into danger

- When Moses was born, Egypt's Pharaoh decreed that all the baby **Israelite** boys be put to death. The Israelites were growing fast and Pharaoh wanted to stop that.

- When Jesus was born, Herod, the local Roman-appointed "king," ordered all the baby boys under two years old to be killed. He thought the new Messiah would threaten his rule.

- In both cases, a lot of other baby boys died, but these two were spared.

> **Hebrews/Israelites/Jews** names for God's chosen people—the people responsible for writing most of the Bible

Born after 400 years of waiting

- The Israelites lived in Egypt for around 400 years. During that time, they became slaves and prayed for God to return them to their homeland—that's when Moses was born.

- For 400 years before Jesus, God had not called any prophets to speak to the Israelites. Many prayed and waited for God to speak. Finally, Jesus was born.

The Bigger Story

The book of the Bible called "Hebrews" explains a lot of ways Jesus is greater than Moses. *Look up Hebrews 1:1–4 as an example.*

- **How did God speak in the times before Jesus?**
- **How does he speak "in these last days," days when Jesus was on Earth?**
- **What else do these verses say about Jesus?**

Remember God's promise to Moses about the Prophet to come—that he would speak exactly what God told him to say? God spoke to everyone through Jesus. Jesus said, "I don't speak on my own authority. The Father who sent me has commanded me what to say and how to say it" (John 12:49). Jesus was the Prophet who spoke only what God told him to say. He did only what God showed him to do. He did this to show people what God is like and to prove he is God's Son.

Hebrews tells us that Jesus is also the one who made the universe. He is the "heir"—the one who will inherit everything. That's because he not only made it, but he **redeemed** what he had made when he died on the cross and rose again.

> **Redeem**
> to buy back, to get ownership of something again, in exchange for a payment

What did an angel say about Jesus' name? Read Matthew 1:20–21 to find out. Jesus is the Savior who would save people from their sin. And he would also fulfill God's ultimate plan—to save the whole world! So, Jesus is both the Prophet and Savior. And everything is doubly his inheritance!

What's That Mean to Me?

Moses is impressive, right? But the "Moses Plan" was just a little part of the huge, eternal plan God has for us (and for the whole world) through Jesus. *How long has God had this planned? Read Ephesians 1:3–4 to find out!*

Before God created the world, he had already planned for Jesus to be the center of the universe. Jesus made it. He holds it together right now. He redeemed it. *What does 2 Corinthians 5:18–19 tell us he is doing now?* Jesus is **reconciling** all of it to God the Father! Before God made the world, he had already planned for Jesus to take the punishment for your sin so that you could know God and be part of his kingdom. And God has amazing plans for your life! We need to pay attention—looking and listening for him to reveal his plans. We'll learn more about that soon.

> **Reconcile**
> restoring peace and friendship between two people who have argued

Week 1 • Day 2

Your Turn

What are two ways that Jesus is like Moses? What are two ways he is greater than Moses?

1.

2.

Think about a time you were mad at someone, but then became friends again. How did it feel to reconcile?

What is something you saw today that reminded you of God's love for you? (If you didn't see anything, then go take a walk and look!)

Prayer

God, what you do is _____.

Thanks for _____
_____.

Thank you that you were thinking of me even before
_____
_____.

I know your plans for me are _____.
(See Jeremiah 29:11.)

Help me to pay attention to what you are saying. It's easy to be distracted!

In Jesus' name, amen.

Week 1 • Day 3

Tell Me the Timeline

Over the next few weeks, you are going to learn a lot about Moses and Jesus. To keep things straight, create a timeline of their lives.

What You'll Need

- scissors
- paper, several sheets
- tape
- markers

What You'll Do

1. Cut several sheets of paper in half lengthwise and tape them together end-to-end on one side.

2. Flip the connected pages over. This is your timeline sheet.

3. Copy the icons, dates and the words in order.

4. Put space between the icons. That helps show approximately how much time was in between the dates that are listed.

5. Remember that before the birth of Jesus, the numbers of the dates go from larger to smaller. And all dates are approximate.

6. Add other dates and create icons for other history points you think are important. There has been a lot of history since 95 A.D.!

God creates the world	Before 4000 B.C.
Noah survives the flood	2500 B.C.
Abraham settles in Canaan	2075 B.C.
Jacob (Israel) and family move to Egypt	1875 B.C.
Israelites are slaves in Egypt	1600 B.C.
Moses is born	1525 B.C.
Israelites leave Egypt with Moses	1446 B.C.
God gives the Law	1445 B.C.
Moses dies; Israelites enter Canaan	1405 B.C.
David becomes King	1010 B.C.
Solomon builds Temple	959 B.C.
Israelites (northern) taken to Assyria	722 B.C.
Israelites (southern) taken to Babylon	585 B.C.
Israelites (southern) resettle their land	515 B.C.
400 years without a prophet	—
Jesus is born	5 B.C.
Jesus is baptized	26 A.D.
Jesus dies and rises again	30 A.D.
The Holy Spirit comes	30 A.D.
Letter to the Hebrews written	68 A.D.
Revelation written	95 A.D.

Week 1 • Day 4

Looking for Jesus

As slaves in Egypt the Israelites "cried out" to the Lord for freedom—they prayed!

Hundreds of years later, under the Roman rule, the Israelites "cried out" to the Lord, too. They were looking for God to send the **Messiah** or "Chosen One," the world's Savior from sin. *God promised someone that he would see the Messiah before he died. What was his name? Read Luke 2:25–26.*

The Holy Spirit brought Simeon into the Temple court at the very moment Mary and Joseph walked in with baby Jesus. *What three things did Simeon say about Jesus? Read them in Luke 2:30–32.* Simeon had waited and waited for God's Messiah. And now, he saw him with his own eyes!

Anna was looking for the Messiah, too (see Luke 2:36-38). She was very old—she had fasted and prayed in the Temple for years. She'd been expecting, noticing, looking for this baby—so, when she came into the Temple courts, she was delighted! HERE he was, the one she had looked for! She thanked and praised God and told everyone around, "HERE is the Messiah, the one who will **redeem** Israel!"

Simeon and Anna were looking for Jesus! They didn't know his name. They didn't know when they would meet him, or how, but they were expecting him!

> **Messiah**
> the promised or expected savior

> **Redeem**
> to buy back, to get ownership of something again, in exchange for a payment

Some people like to share God's work in their lives. They may say, "That's a God-story" or "This is a God thing!" But if we're going to have a "God-story" to tell, we must first be LOOKING to see where God is at work. It's easy for us to forget to look! We can ask for God to help us notice, and then begin to look for God's help. We can expect to see him come to help us, the way Simeon and Anna looked for Jesus!

Sometimes we want to tell God HOW to help. But that's just silly! We really do NOT know how God should do his job! But we can always ask for and expect God's help. We can look for things around us that show us what Jesus is doing—events that say, "God is up to something here!"

What might be a clue or sign that God is at work?

- **Maybe you're not afraid of something you used to be afraid of.**
- **Maybe you now are kind to people you used to make fun of.**
- **Perhaps you now tell the truth when you used to lie a lot.**

Think about it. Those all show God is at work in your life. Like Simeon and Anna, we need to pay attention! When we're asking God for help and looking for what he is doing, this makes us ready to face our future and think about the plans God already has for us.

Your Turn

What is exciting about following Jesus?

What's a way you've noticed Jesus at work in you or in others?

What clues do you already have about something God may want you to do in the future? Something he wants you to do right now?

What helps you to pay attention and notice what God is doing?

Week 1 • Day 5

Family Quilt

Names can link families together across generations. Everyone's family is different. Some people have many siblings and some have none. Some live with grandparents and some are adopted. The people in your family impact your life every day. You were woven together like the threads of a quilt. Make your own family quilt to show who makes up your family.

What You'll Need

- heavy paper
- ruler
- pencils
- scissors
- butcher paper
- markers
- glue
- tape

What You'll Do

1. Use a ruler and pencil to draw a grid on butcher paper with 8x8-inch squares. This will be your quilt template. Make sure there is at least one square in the grid for each family member.

2. Cut heavy paper into 8x8-inch squares, making at least one for each family member.

3. Each person designs and colors their own quilt square or squares. Doodle, decorate, draw pictures of things you like or write words about God's plan in your life.

4. Make more than one square if you have time and ideas! If you have pets, make squares for them, too!

5. Lay out the finished squares on your template (from step 1). Move them around to see what arrangements looks best.

6. Glue finished squares onto the butcher paper grid to make a family quilt. Display the paper quilt by taping it to a wall. Talk about how each family member decorated their squares. Find out the stories behind each person's decorations.

Prayer

Dear God, your Word says you have good plans for me. Help me to be looking for your help and listening for your plans. Help me to trust you, so that I obey you. In Jesus' name, amen.

Week 1 • Day 6

Plan a Trip

God planned for his people to have their own land one day. The Promised Land was named Israel after the patriarch, Israel, who was also called Jacob. If you could name a country after yourself, what would you call it? Write it on the line below.

_____

What would your country look like? Is it beachy or snowy? Draw a picture below.

If someone were planning a trip to your country what would they need to bring? Make a list below.

_____
_____
_____

Bonus: Sticky Futures

Parts of the future can be exciting. Other parts may be scary. But the best part is that God has good plans for us! What do you think God might have you do in the future? Play this fun game to talk about future careers with your friends and family.

What You'll Need

- Post-it Notes in three colors
- Pens or pencils

What You'll Do

1. Give each player one of each color of sticky note and a pen or pencil.

2. On the agreed-on color (ex: blue), each player writes an occupation.

3. On another agreed-on color (ex: pink), each player writes a place.

4. On the third color (ex: yellow), each player writes an activity.

5. After everyone has finished their three notes, sit in a circle. Each player passes the blue note to their left, the pink note to the person on their right, and then gives the yellow note to any other person.

6. Take turns to put the words on your notes into this sentence: "In the future, I will work as (blue/occupation) in (pink/place) and will enjoy (yellow/activity)."

7. Pass the notes again, and see what other sticky futures you may come up with!

Week 2 • Day 1

Protected by God

I wait quietly before God, for my victory comes from him. He alone is my rock and my salvation, my fortress where I will never be shaken . . . O my people, trust in him at all times. Pour out your heart to him, for God is our refuge.

PSALM 62:1-2, 8

God is our refuge and strength, always ready to help in times of trouble.

PSALM 46:1

Astonishing Protection

EXODUS 2:11-25; MATTHEW 2

Surprising Similarities

Royal favor

- The princess of Egypt found Moses in the Nile River and raised him as a prince in Pharaoh's palace.

- When Jesus was young, the wise men gave him gifts fit for kings—gold, frankincense and myrrh!

Not My Dad

- In the palace, Moses was not raised by his natural father.

> Read Hebrews 5:5 to find out what God the Father said about Jesus.

- Jesus' natural father wasn't Joseph, it was God. Jesus was also brought up by a man who wasn't his father.

Run to Safety

- As an adult, Moses watched an Egyptian slave master beat an Israelite slave. He got boiling mad at this cruelty. So, he beat the slave master badly—and killed him and hid the body. When Pharaoh found out, he planned to kill Moses! But God protected Moses and he escaped to safety in Midian.

- When Herod wanted to kill Jesus, God protected him and sent him away to Egypt to hide him and save his life. *Read Matthew 2:14–15 to discover what the prophet said about this, long before Jesus came to Earth.*

The Bigger Story

God's protection covered Jesus and Moses throughout their lives. After Jesus was born, the wise men came to Jerusalem looking for the "King of the Jews." They were astronomers who had seen a new star that convinced them to find this king! Herod was the Roman-appointed "king of the Jews" at that time. He'd already killed most of his family, fearing they might take his throne. *How did Herod feel about this news? Find out in Matthew 2:3–6.* Now Herod knew the town where Jesus was born. He told the wise men to find the young child and to let him know where to find him.

The wise men found Jesus and worshiped him. They honored the little child with expensive gifts. But that night, the wise men were warned in a dream not to go back to Herod. God also directed Joseph to take Jesus and Mary to Egypt—right then! Quickly and quietly, under the cover of darkness, off they went. In his anger, Herod killed many other baby boys in that area. *What prophet had predicted this awful event? Read Matthew 2:17–18 to find out.*

Joseph, Mary, and Jesus stayed in Egypt until Herod died. Then God sent an angel to tell Joseph it was safe to come back. But when Joseph heard that the new Herod was as bad as the old one, he decided to go north. *Where did they go? Read Matthew 2:23 to see.*

God protected Moses all his life—first through the princess, and then by keeping him safe in Midian. Keeping Moses safe was one part of God's even GREATER plan! *Read Hebrews 2:14–15 to find out why we don't have to be afraid of death anymore.*

God protected both Moses and Jesus *from* death, keeping them safe until just the right time, so that they could fulfill their part in God's plan. And then Jesus, *through* death—by dying on the cross—destroyed the devil, who held the power of death that makes us humans so afraid. That proves Jesus can do ANYTHING!

What's That Mean to Me?

Some of us have lived through scary times. Some of us have never had anything scary happen. Everyone's life is different. But one thing is the same: Whether your life has felt scary or safe, God has been protecting you.

He listens when you ask him for help. He is on your side! He has a perfect time and way to guide and guard your life. He proved he can do anything when he destroyed the enemy's power. He is like that fortress in the photo—can you imagine how well protected you would be there? God's protection is far better! He will protect you, help you and show you what to do when you ask him!

Your Turn

What's one way Moses' and Jesus' stories are alike?

What do you think is the biggest difference between what Moses did and what Jesus did?

When have you felt like you were in danger? What did you do? What did God do?

Prayer

Try this multiple-choice prayer and circle one word in each parenthesis. Then read the prayer aloud to God!

Dear God,

Sometimes I feel like I'm (alone, afraid, not accepted). Some things make me (nervous, anxious, scared).

Please help me to remember that you care about me when I need (help, protection, comfort). I can always pray to you.

When I feel like I don't know whether I should (run, hide, fight) or (scream, cry, freeze), help me to (trust, rest, believe) in you.

Thank you that you can do anything! In Jesus' name, amen.

Week 2 • Day 3

Escape Route

When baby Jesus was in danger, God warned Joseph to move the family to Egypt. You may not need to leave the country to be safe, like Jesus did, but there are other emergencies that can surprise us. Earthquakes, floods, tornadoes, hurricanes, mudslides, fires—which of these is the most likely to happen where you live? Have you ever made an escape or emergency plan for yourself and your family? People who have a plan for what to do are better off—and are quicker to help others.

What You'll Need

- small sheets of poster board (9x12 inch) (alternately, a ring-bound sketch pad)
- permanent markers in several colors
- hole punch
- binder ring

What You'll Do

1. Call a family meeting. Talk about the kinds of emergencies your family might need a plan for.

2. Ask an adult to take notes on the things you agree upon. For instance, if there is a fire in your house, agree upon an outside place where everyone will safely meet.

3. Use one sheet of poster board for each kind of emergency. Write down what the family agrees upon doing in case of that emergency—fire, earthquake, etc.

4. Draw a map of your house and yard on the same poster board. Draw colored lines to show what the escape route is in case of that emergency.

5. When you have completed a plan for each kind of escape, punch a hole in the corner of each poster board and put the binder ring through the holes.

6. Hang them in a place where everyone can find these instructions.

Remember—God is our refuge and our fortress. The first step in any emergency is to ask for his help!

Week 2 • Day 4

Learning to Rest

I wait quietly before God, for my victory comes from him. He alone is my rock and my salvation, my fortress where I will never be shaken . . . O my people, trust in him at all times. Pour out your heart to him, for God is our refuge.

PSALM 62:1-2,8

What is resting?

Is resting that horrible thing they used to make you do in kindergarten, forcing you to lie still—and you weren't sleepy?

Or is resting more than just not moving?

Maybe it looks like:

- Not hurrying
- Not worrying
- Not trying to figure out what to do
- Not trying to protect myself
- Not thinking I'm better than someone else
- Taking time to breathe
- Praying and asking God what to do

Our verse today was written by King David who encountered many scary situations. He was confronted by a giant who wanted to kill him. He was chased into caves by his father-in-law, King Saul—who also wanted to kill him. David had his share of truly scary times and daring escapes! It's kind of strange to think that someone could be restful on the inside when he was hiding or running away from enemy soldiers or hateful rulers!

List four ways you like to rest:

1. _____   3. _____

2. _____   4. _____

Resting in God is a lot like sitting wherever you are sitting right now, reading this. Are you nervous that the bed might fall apart? Are you worrying that the chair might collapse? That the floor might break? Unless you are in an earthquake right now, probably not! You're fully resting your body in the chair or the sofa or the bed. You're not even thinking about whether what you're resting on will

hold you up. Your body is in a position of full trust!

How can you learn to practice resting?

- Learn the verses for this week. Say them aloud to yourself when you get that urge to run, scream, or panic.

- Practice taking a deep breath. Let it go while you ask God what you need to know about the thing that is scaring you.

- Ask him to give you wisdom because God promises to answer you!

This is what James tells us:

> *If you need wisdom, ask our generous God, and he will give it to you. He will not rebuke you for asking. But when you ask him, be sure that your faith is in God alone. Do not waver, for a person with divided loyalty is as unsettled as a wave of the sea that is blown and tossed by the wind.*
>
> **JAMES 1:5-6**

So when you ask God for wisdom, expect him to answer you. Then, when you know what to do, just do it—don't doubt. You can trust that if God will give you wisdom, then he'll also help you do what you need to do. No hurry, no worry, just rest!

Your Turn

Draw a picture of a place that feels safe to you.
Then draw yourself in that safe place.

Week 2 • Day 5

Shake Up Salt

Psalm 62 talks about God being our rock and our comfort in times of trouble. Salt is made up of very tiny rock crystals. Today, make salt art depicting a place you feel safe to remember that God will always protect you.

What You'll Need

- table salt
- black paper
- pencil
- watercolors
- paintbrushes
- white glue
- cookie sheet and tray

Optional: May use food coloring and an eye dropper in place of watercolors and paintbrushes.

What You'll Do

1. Lay the black paper on a cookie sheet and tray. This helps with clean up later.

2. In pencil, draw a place that makes you feel safe. It could be your bed, your treehouse, church, school, or wherever.

3. Trace the pencil marks with glue. Make the glue lines thick.

4. Shake the salt over the glue until it covers the whole drawing.

5. Tilt the paper so that the excess salt falls onto the tray.

6. Ensure paintbrushes are very wet with color. Lightly paint over the salt. Be gentle with the brush, or it will it will move the salt out of place.

7. Let dry.

Week 2 • Day 6

Hideouts

This recipe is simple and fun to make. The marshmallows disappear once you cook the dough leaving a "cave" in the middle! While you work, talk about how God is like a hiding place. Tell stories about ways he has helped you and your family.

What You'll Need

- 16 marshmallows
- ½ cup (1 stick) butter, melted
- ¼ cup sugar
- 2 tablespoons cinnamon
- 2 (8-ounce) cans of crescent-roll dough

What You'll Do

1. Mix sugar and cinnamon in a small bowl.

2. On a baking sheet, unroll crescent-roll dough. Separate each roll along the dotted lines.

3. Roll marshmallows in melted butter, and then in cinnamon-sugar mixture. Tip: To avoid messy hands, skewer the marshmallow on a corn holder.

4. Set a coated marshmallow in the middle of an unrolled crescent dough segment.

5. Roll the dough around the marshmallow until it is completely covered. Push in the sides as you go.

6. Pinch seams on either end to seal each roll. Make sure the marshmallow is completely covered by the dough. If not, the marshmallow will seep out while baking.

7. Place rolls on a baking sheet, and bake at 375°F for about 12 minutes.

8. After removing rolls from the oven, brush with remaining melted butter and then sprinkle with remaining cinnamon-sugar mixture. Serve warm.

Prayer

Dear God,

When I don't feel safe, when I am not sure of what to do, please remind me to ask you first. To stop and breathe and listen for the wisdom you promise to give. Then help me to do what you give me wisdom to do. Thank you. In Jesus' name, amen.

Week 3 • Day 1

Called by God

No one lights a lamp and then puts it under a basket. Instead, a lamp is placed on a stand, where it gives light to everyone in the house. In the same way let your good deeds shine out for all to see so that everyone will praise your heavenly Father.

MATTHEW 5:15-16

We are God's masterpiece. He has created us anew in Christ Jesus, so we can do the good things he planned for us long ago.

EPHESIANS 2:10

The Perfect Job

EXODUS 3:1-4:31; MATTHEW 3:13-16; 5:14-16

Surprising Similarities

Exiles Returned

- Moses was in **exile** in a foreign land (Midian) until a new the Pharaoh was ruling.

- Jesus stayed in exile in a foreign land (Egypt) until a new Herod was ruling.

> **Exile**
> To be kept from living in your own country, usually because of political reasons or to punish someone

A Sign That "It's Time"

- The burning bush was God's sign to Moses. It was time to free the Israelites.

- The Holy Spirit descending like a dove was God's sign for Jesus to begin his ministry.

From Royal to Humble

- Moses lived like royalty in Egypt in the palace. He left his position of power so he could save the Israelite slaves.

- Jesus was (and is) royalty in Heaven, but he left his position and his rights as king to save the world that was in slavery to sin.

> **Fasting**
> Not eating; going without food. Jesus fasted so he could focus on God and spend more time praying to him

Desert Days

- Moses spent forty years in the deserts of Midian.

- Jesus spent forty days **fasting** in the desert.

- Both times were preparation for a big job!

For forty years, Moses lived far from Egypt. He became a shepherd, a husband and a dad. It doesn't seem like shepherding would prepare anyone for freeing slaves, does it? But God used it! *What did God tell Moses to do? Read Exodus 3:10.* Herding sheep taught him a lot about leadership—and Moses also learned the area around Mount Sinai, where he would later lead God's people! *How did God show Moses that he would be with Moses? Read Exodus 4:1–5 to find out.* Moses realized that if God can change his stick into a snake, then he can help Moses free the Israelites.

The Bigger Story

Moses' history-making job was a BIG deal. But we all know that Jesus' job was FAR bigger! *How did God show Jesus that he would be with him? Find out by reading John 1:32–34.* God the Father sent his Holy Spirit like a dove to rest on Jesus. It was a sign that God would give Jesus all the power he needed to do the world's GREATEST job! After Jesus was baptized by John, he began telling people about the Kingdom of God.

What did Jesus say about the work he did? Read John 8:28–29 to see. Jesus never did anything because HE thought it was a good idea. That's why Jesus is the ONLY perfect sacrifice to take away sin—because he never went off on his own to do HIS thing.

Jesus had something important to tell people about THEIR job, too! When some people asked him, "What work do we have to do in order to do what God wants?" Jesus answered them, "This is the 'work' or job God has for you to do: to believe in the one he has sent" (see John 6:29).

The people who asked Jesus this question were used to doing "good works," or religious things they thought pleased God.

But those weren't the jobs God wanted them to do. That's why Jesus said they had only ONE JOB—to believe in him! When we believe in Jesus FIRST, it is easier to do the work he has for us.

What's That Mean to Me?

If you're part of God's family, if you believe in Jesus, then you're ready to start looking for that next job God has for you! God's kids don't just sit around the palace. God has good things for you to do right now and in your future, as well. Like Moses, the things you do now will prepare you for jobs assignments later!

Remember: If you've never believed in Jesus, it doesn't matter what other good things you do—you're doing it backwards. It may look good, but God calls those kinds of actions "self-righteousness"and he says self-righteousness is like filthy rags. Yuck! Only when our good actions come from love for Jesus and are powered by God's Spirit do our "good works" please God.

So, our first job is to believe in Jesus. Then we ask God, and listen for what God wants us to do next! We don't rely on our own smarts or ability. Then we believe he will help us to do it, the same way he helped Moses and Jesus!

Week 3 • Day 2

Your Turn

What are some "good works" you have seen people do?

What makes a "good work" different for followers of Jesus?

Why do you think our inner thoughts matter to God?

Prayer

What would you tell a friend about a recent "good work" you did?

_____

_____

_____

_____

How did you please God in this job? Remember that job ONE is to believe in Jesus, and job TWO is how you thought and felt on the inside when you did this job.

_____

_____

_____

_____

_____

_____

Week 3 • Day 3

A "Me" Challenge

God knows us better than we know ourselves. God says we are his "masterpiece" (Ephesians 2:10)! Genesis tells us he created us with his words. So here is today's challenge: Use your words to describe yourself!

I dream about

_____

I worry about

_____

I am happy when

_____

I am good at

_____

I don't like to

_____

I feel brave when

_____

I am glad that

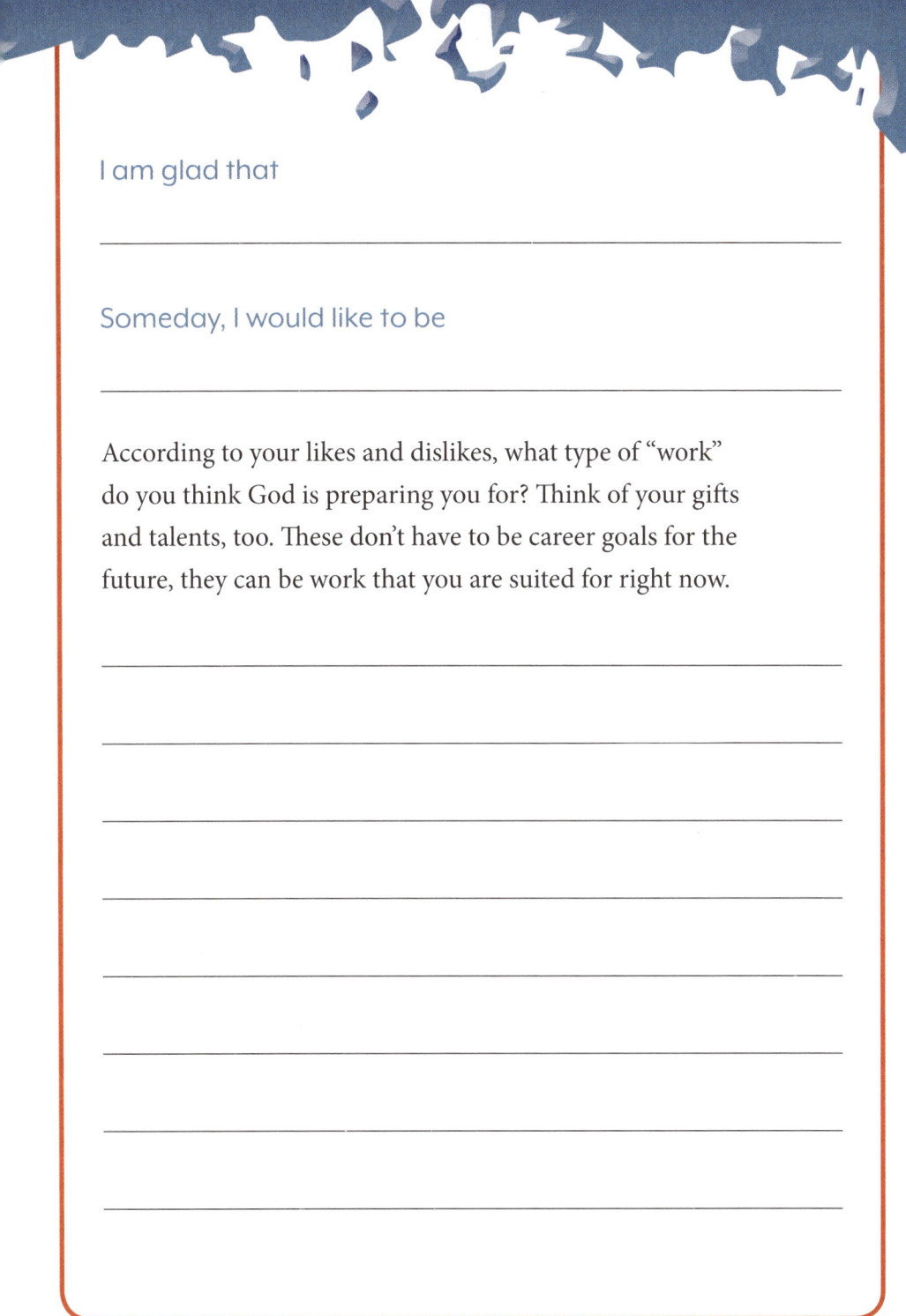

_____

Someday, I would like to be

_____

According to your likes and dislikes, what type of "work" do you think God is preparing you for? Think of your gifts and talents, too. These don't have to be career goals for the future, they can be work that you are suited for right now.

_____

_____

_____

_____

_____

_____

_____

Week 3 • Day 4

Selfie Service

Ever since we've had mobile phones with cameras, people have been taking selfies. Selfies are often taken by people doing something "good"—maybe giving something to a homeless person or helping at a clean-up day. Those are good things to do. But Jesus said that WHY we do good things matters more to God than the "good work" itself.

What did Jesus call people who believe in and follow him in Matthew 5:13–16? We are the "salt of the earth" and the "light of the world." Let's think about those two things. First, salt is not something you use by itself. It's useful only *in relationship* to something else. It makes food taste better. It keeps things from rotting (like salted meat) and can cleanse a wound or sore (although it really hurts!).

Light is also something that isn't so good just by itself. Ever been "blinded by the light"? ACK! But light matters *in relationship* to something else. When you need to walk down the hall at night, a teeny night light keeps you from stubbing your toe!

So, salt and light are very important—but they are important *in their relationship* to other things.

In the same way, Jesus says we are important—but that our "good deeds" are about our relationship to God. We don't do them to get attention for ourselves, but to "throw light" on God. The reason to do it is so that those who saw what we did will "glorify (praise) GOD," not us!

If we do good things so that we can take a selfie, get a reward, or get noticed—or do it out of our own strength, the "good deed" may look the same OUTSIDE, but we're doing a good thing for a wrong reason INSIDE. And God cares about the INSIDE reason!

What did Jesus say about how we give to the poor in Matthew 6:1–3? WHAT? So secret, that one hand doesn't even notice that the other hand is giving? Jesus called those people who crave attention for themselves "hypocrites" or fakes. Outside, they look SO good and kind and spiritual. But in their hearts they say, "See me! See me! See the good thing I am doing!"

Jesus says, "Those people got their reward. They don't need to expect any reward from God." Like posting that good-deed selfie on social media—you can go for everyone's approval; but that's all the reward you get. Don't expect God's approval or reward.

What did Jesus say in Matthew 6:4 about the way God will reward us? We don't know what God will do to reward us, but one day, he will reward us! If we don't make a big deal out of the things we do, but do them so that they point to him and not us, Jesus says that job is worth doing! When our actions come from love for Jesus, when they are powered by God's Spirit, and when our desire is to "throw light on" God so that people will praise him—those "good works" please God.

And when you think you don't have the strength or smarts to do a job God wants you to do, remember, he believes you can do it. He makes you able! So no worries! When God gives you a job, take time to think of a way to do it that won't show you off, but will show off God. It will be more fun and it will feel different—try it, you'll like it! So will God!

Your Turn

Everyone works. Everyone has jobs they do. Right now, being a student may be your main job.

In the space below, brainstorm some ways you could do your job so that people notice GOD and praise him. Write or draw your ideas.

Week 3 • Day 5

Zero to Hero

Everyone has a job to do. It's not always about the KIND of job you do, but the WAY in which you do it, that honors and "shines the light" on God. Read a few "job-related" back stories you may not know! See if you can match the person to the description. Write the correct description number under each photo and name on the right.

1. Some of this person's teachers doubted they would ever complete school; this person failed part of a school entrance exam. But by working on what was possible and asking questions, this person's name is now a synonym for "genius."

2. Mostly home schooled, due to deafness from a fever. This did not dampen a love for reading and experimenting—and today we know this person as the inventor of movies, electric lights, and over 10,000 other inventions!

3. What can you do when you break your neck? You might think not much. But this person decided to find a way to do something! They learned to paint by holding a brush between their teeth! Now they're a famous artist, speaker and advocate for those with disabilities.

4. Growing famous was easy for this composer. Growing deaf was not. But this did not stop the music! This composer continued to write music even after growing deaf, often laying an ear to piano to pick up the vibrations!

Answers on Page 220

THOMAS EDISON

JONI EARECKSON TADA

_____

_____

LUDWIG VAN BEETHOVEN

ALBERT EINSTEIN

_____

_____

Week 3 • Day 6

Talk About Work

Jesus told us that when we do something—even something that impresses other people—it only pleases God if we do it for the right reasons and with the right ATTITUDE.

Today, interview a person you know who is over fifty years old. (Yes, the person needs to be OLD!) Ask some or all the questions provided.

If you're asking an older relative, you might want to take notes, or even record the conversation on a phone and upload it. That way, everyone in your family can hear the stories and learn from them!

Interview Questions

- What jobs have you done in your life?
- What job did you dislike the most?
- Why did you dislike that job?
- What made the disliked job easier to do?
- What caused you to change jobs?
- What job did you like a lot?
- What made you enjoy that job?
- Did you ever feel like you did a job in a way that honored God?

- When we work, what do you think makes people notice God instead of us?

- In what ways did you feel you were pleasing or honoring God in your work?

- What things do you think makes jobs or work pleasing to God?

- What is something you did that you weren't paid to do? Why did you do it?

- In what ways did you feel like you were "paid" for doing that, besides money?

Prayer

Dear God, I want to learn now the right way to work, no matter what job I do.

Please help me learn _____ and _____ in whatever I do.

Help me learn how to help people notice YOU, instead of learning how to make ME look good. That's the best job I can ever have. In Jesus' name, amen.

Week 4 • Day 1

Made Strong by God

But you will receive power when the Holy Spirit comes upon you. And you will be my witnesses, telling people about me everywhere—in Jerusalem, throughout Judea, in Samaria, and to the ends of the earth.

ACTS 1:8

Don't be afraid, for I am with you. Don't be discouraged, for I am your God. I will strengthen you and help you. I will hold you up with my victorious right hand.

ISAIAH 41:10

Power and Authority
EXODUS 5:1–6:10; MATTHEW 4:17,23-25; ACTS 1:1-11

Surprising Similarities

Convincing Miracles!

- Supernatural **miracles** showed everyone in Egypt that God was with Moses and that he was telling the truth.

- Jesus' many miracles proved God was with him, that he is God's Son, and that he was telling the truth.

> **Miracles**
> things that happen which can't be explained by natural or scientific laws; acts of God which go above natural laws

Water Wonders!

- Moses turned water into blood to show Pharaoh that God had sent him.

- Jesus turned water into wine to show people that he was sent by God and that he can do anything, just like God his Father!

Power in the Blood!

- Egyptians depended upon the water of the Nile River to live. Moses turned their source of life-water into blood to show them God has power.

- Jesus *gave* his blood so that all people could have what he called "living water"—eternal life with him!

When Moses first faced Pharaoh, he had to prove that letting the Israelites go was God's idea, not his own! *How did Moses and his brother, Aaron, show that God was with them? Read Exodus 7:8–12 to find one example.* God's power was clearly greater than the power of the Egyptians! But God had already told Moses that Pharaoh would harden his heart and would not listen. So even when Moses turned the water of the Nile into blood, Pharaoh didn't change. His heart was hard!

The Bigger Story

Moses did many more miracles—the rest of his life was a series of miracles! But Jesus' life tells a bigger story. We can't count miracles to decide who's greater. *Why does John say that would be impossible? Read John 21:25 to find out!* The number of Jesus' miracles far outweighs Moses' miracles!

Why did Jesus do miracles?

First, to show everyone what God is like!

- Jesus stopped storms—to show he can protect us.
- He sent evil spirits away—to show he has power over the devil and evil spirits.
- He healed sick people—to show he is stronger than illness.
- He fed hungry people—to show how to be a servant.
- He even made dead people alive—to show he is more powerful than death.

Second, Jesus also showed everyone that he is God's own Son, the Messiah or Anointed One. He showed that he did not do anything without God the Father's **authority**.

> **Authority**
> the power or right to give orders and make decisions, given by someone who is of a higher status (God, in this case)

But Jesus promised his friends that they would do even greater things. *Read Acts 1:8 to find out why.* The Holy Spirit made it possible for us to access the same power that Jesus showed when he lived on Earth. Then we can spread the good news of God's love to everyone! After the Holy Spirit came (*Read Acts 2 for the whole story*), Jesus' friends did many miracles. Best of all, they had the power to love each other in the way Jesus told them to love!

What's That Mean to Me?

Because the Holy Spirit came—and is still here—we can trust God to help us with his power! You may not do amazing miracles, but it does amaze people when you love those who are mean to you. It does make a difference when you kindly share with people who need something, without trying to be noticed. Your actions are showing others that you belong to God. He is the one who can make us able to love unlovable people and do things that are hard to do—unless he helps us!

- God will help you to be kind—that's the power of love!

- He promises to help you know the smartest thing to do when you ask him—that's the power of wisdom!

- He'll give you the power to keep on loving and keep on waiting—that's the power of patience and persistence!

What does he say he will give you in Philippians 4:19? He will give you everything you need! God has the power you need for every situation!

Week 4 • Day 2

Your Turn

What did the miracles show Pharaoh and the Egyptians about God?

What did the miracles show to the people of Jesus' day about God?

In your life, what shows you that God is making a difference inside you?

What shows others that you are under God's authority?

Prayer

Write the phrases in the Word Bank on the appropriate blanks. Then read the prayer aloud!

Word Bank
with you
hard to love
me, too
easy to love

Dear Jesus,

Your miracles proved that God was _____.

I want to show that God is with _____.

Help me show your love to people who are _____.

And show your love to those who are _____.

I need your power in my life to do that. Amen.

Week 4 • Day 3

YOU-nique Contribution

Moses and Jesus both made unique contributions—each did jobs no one else could do. Notice God didn't set a sign beside the burning bush that said, "In search of a willing volunteer." Moses wasn't even a good speaker—and that was why God chose him! WHAT? *Because* he wasn't good at it? Let that sink in!

A wise man once said, "God doesn't call the qualified. He qualifies the called!" In other words, if God tells you to do it, he'll make you able to do it. He does this so that it is clear that he is working through you. You are not able to do it on your own strength, but because God is with you.

Today, have some fun with your own uniqueness. No one on earth has a fingerprint exactly like yours.

What You'll Need

- soft pencil
- paper
- wipes
- magnifying glass

What You'll Do

1. Draw a 1-inch square on the paper. Fill it in. Be sure to press hard with the pencil.

2. Rub your pointer finger over the penciled area.

3. Roll your finger over an empty area of the paper.

4. Use the magnifying glass to see the details or zoom in with your camera.

5. Invite family members or friends to try it, too. See if you can guess whose fingerprints are whose after you have gathered some! Keep your fingerprint paper and use it as your "stamp pad."

6. Now, make more fingerprints! Make prints from various fingers to create an illustration of you doing something that is unique to you—maybe you're good at holding open doors for people, or making people laugh, or being kind to animals. (If you want colored fingerprints, use water-based markers and clean your fingers after each color!)

Remember, God has something for you to do that is just for you—that only you can do!

Week 4 • Day 4

Growing Confident

Before Jesus was arrested, his friend Peter promised Jesus that he would never deny him. Peter meant that he was not ashamed to be Jesus' friend. By not denying him, he promised to support Jesus. But Peter chickened out after Jesus was arrested. People asked Peter, "Aren't you Jesus' friend?"

"No, I am not." He told them three times, "I have never met that man."

Mark 14:72 says that afterward, Peter wept bitterly. He was a chicken and he knew it.

After Jesus rose again, he told his friends not to worry about what was going to happen. He said, "Instead, you will receive power when the Holy Spirit comes. And then you'll be my witnesses starting here, and going out all over this country, and then all over the earth!" (That's from our Bible verse for the week, by the way!) And soon after that, Jesus went back to heaven.

Forty days later, just as Jesus had promised, God's Holy Spirit came. What happened to Peter after that? Peter became bold as a lion! He preached to thousands of people and told them about Jesus the Messiah. *Look at Acts 2:41 to find out how many people believed on that day!*

What a difference! *Read Acts 3:6–7 to see what happened to a man who had always been unable to walk.*

The Holy Spirit gave Peter and the other friends of Jesus power to do things they had never thought they would do!

If you are a child of God, a follower of Jesus, then God's Holy Spirit is inside you, too! The Holy Spirit helps us do things we thought we never could do, too! *Now read Hebrews 4:16 to find out what we can expect when we come to God's "throne of grace."*

God promises that he will never leave us. That's why we can be confident when we pray to him—and why we can do things we never thought we could do. God is at work inside us—and he will make us able!

BOLD as a

Your Turn

What is one thing you know about praying?

What is one thing you know about the Holy Spirit?

What is the thing you like best about being part of God's kingdom?

Prayer

Dear God, I am glad that I can pray to you. Thank you for listening to me and thank you for helping me through the Holy Spirit. It gives me confidence to know that in every situation, I can come to you first. In Jesus' name, amen.

Week 4 • Day 5

Problems and Promises

On the right side of the page, write down some problems in your life (for example, afraid at night, bullied by a bigger kid, too tired to do homework, etc.)

For every problem you list, find a comforting promise or verse in the Bible.

HOW? First, check to see if your Bible has a concordance. It will list key words and then Bible references. So look for key words in each problem, and then see what you can find in the concordance. You can also search on a Bible site like Bible Gateway.

Instead of just writing down the reference or "address" of the promise, try writing out a little bit of the verse, so that you remember what it says!

Try to think of at least three problems and find three promises!

Week 4 • Day 6

Power Words

Moses and Jesus spoke to crowds of followers. Their words were important because they came from God. Here is a puzzle to help us think about the words we often associate with power and authority.

Across

3. Opposite of weak.

6. Make a person do something that they don't want to do.

7. A person who is in charge of other people.

8. Power or right to give orders and make decisions.

9. The ultimate source of authority.

Down

1. Thing that happens which can't be explained by natural laws; act of God.

2. Speak in front of many people (like in a church).

4. To convince another person.

5. Remote _____. (Hint: what you use to turn on the TV.)

Answers on Page 220

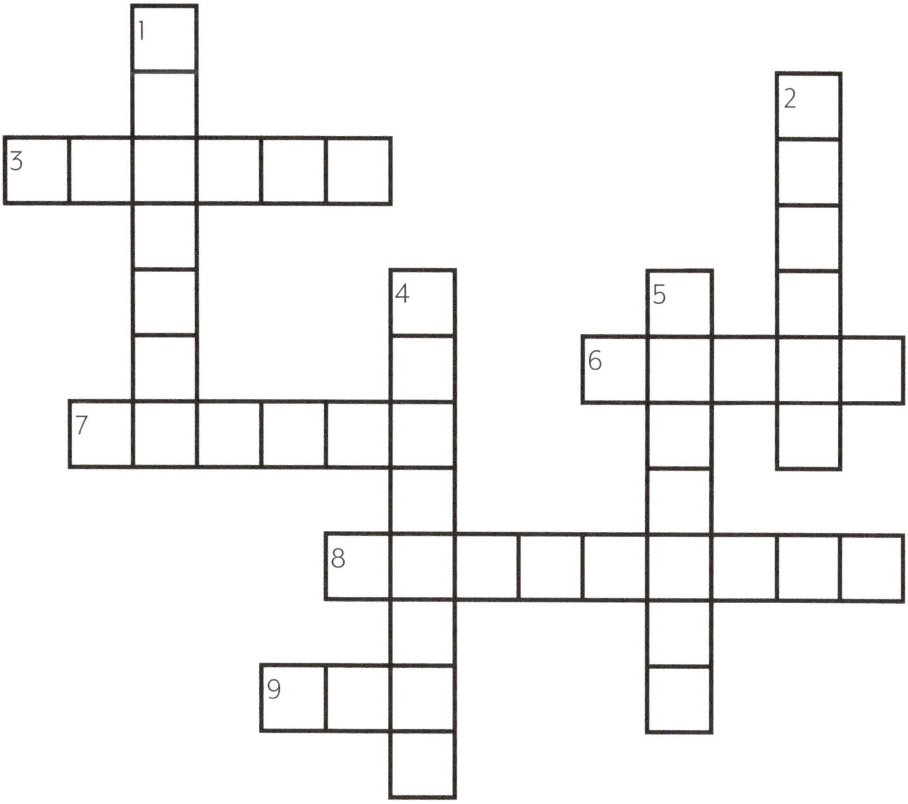
1
2
3
4
5
6
7
8
9

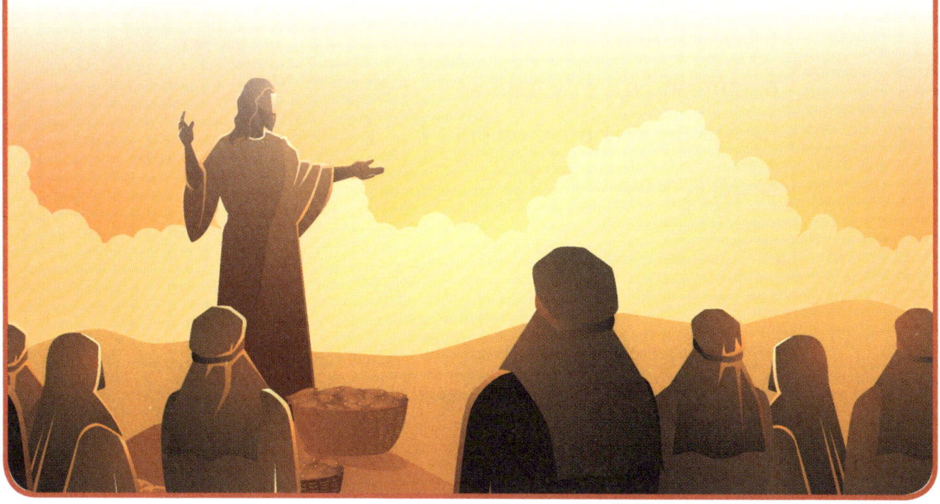

Week 5 • Day 1

Encouraged by God

Even when I walk through the darkest valley, I will not be afraid, for you are close beside me. Your rod and your staff protect and comfort me.

PSALM 23:4

I have told you all this so that you may have peace in me. Here on earth you will have many trials and sorrows. But take heart, because I have overcome the world.

JOHN 16:33

Courage in Chaos
EXODUS 7:1–10:29; MARK 4:35–5:43

Surprising Similarities

Facing Fearful Rulers!

- Moses and Aaron faced Pharaoh and his wise men. Pharaoh knew about God but did not care about God.

- Jesus faced many rulers who knew about God—both religious leaders, and political rulers—but their actions showed they didn't care about God.

Hard Hearts!

- When Moses and Aaron told Pharaoh about each of the troubles God would send, Pharaoh chose to harden his heart. This means he was not understanding toward Moses and his request.

- Jesus was brought before Pilate when he was arrested. Pilate had the choice to either condemn or rescue Jesus from death. Pilate's wife warned him not to punish this innocent man Jesus—but he hardened his heart and condemned Jesus to die.

Face to Face!

- Moses found courage to face fearful situations because he spoke with God " as one speaks to a friend" (Exodus 33:11).

- Jesus' conversations with God caused him to say, "Just as my Father knows me and I know the Father" (John 10:15).

- Both spent time with God, praying and listening to him. This gave them courage to do hard things.

Over and over, Moses and Aaron had to face their fears as they spoke to Pharaoh. It never got easier—every time they told him what God was going to do, Pharaoh got meaner! And the troubles got worse! From blood to frogs to flies to sick animals to invading locusts, to hailstones and darkness—this was chaos! It was only because Moses and Aaron were trusting God and asking God what to do that they could go on! It was scary and dangerous. But let's look at Jesus' danger level!

The Bigger Story

Like Moses, Jesus often talked to angry people! In fact, most rulers got angry at him! But when Jesus spoke to poor people, to the sick or in trouble, or those who knew they were sinners—those people listened to Jesus gladly. They understood him. The self-righteous, educated and important ones often did not.

To find out where Jesus heard the things he said, read John 8:26. He said whatever God told him to say. Why? Because he spent time with God every day. He got up while it was still dark to pray and hear from God.

Then Jesus obeyed God—always. He knew God his Father would do what he said. By fully obeying God, Jesus showed he is God's perfect son. He was perfectly obedient—even when obeying meant he had to die. Jesus even asked God to forgive the angry people who wanted to kill him. He didn't stop because of how it felt. He did this so he could make the way for everyone to join God's kingdom family. That's greater than everything Moses did!

What's That Mean to Me?

Aaron was the High Priest for Moses and the Israelites, but for us, Jesus is our High Priest. *To find out more about Jesus the "new" High Priest, read Hebrews 4:15–16.* Jesus was tempted in every way, just as we are—yet he did not sin! He showed us that we can approach God's throne of grace with confidence, because Jesus understands who we are.

- He understands what we need.

- He has felt every hard feeling we have had.

- He has felt how it feels to be tempted to turn from obeying God and do it our own way.

But he never gave in. He never sinned. That makes him God's perfect High Priest forever. He is always **interceding** for us—praying for us!

That means we can pray with confidence. In the middle of chaos, we can take time to be with God and read God's Word. We can ask God to show us what we need to know and what we need to do. Then, we can listen and obey—because we trust that when God tells us to do something, he will give us the courage we need. He will give us **mercy** and **grace** when we pray. We can be sure that it's OK to tell him everything and to ask him anything—especially things that look scary and impossible to us!

> **Interceding**
> Standing between two sides as a peacemaker or intervening on behalf of another person. Prayer is a way to intercede.

> **Mercy**
> God's compassion or forgiveness toward us.

> **Grace**
> God's freely-given, undeserved kindness.

Week 5 • Day 2

Your Turn

If you were a news reporter for Moses and the Israelites, what are some headlines you would write?

If you were reporting on Jesus and the anger he faced, what are some headlines you would write?

Prayer

What are some "modern-day plagues"—big problems people face? Draw several in the space below. Then read the prayer aloud, filling in the blanks with the "plagues" you illustrated.

God, thank you that you are full of mercy and grace. When _____ happens, when I see people _____ or _____, when I don't know what to do, you promise me wisdom and help. Thank you for confidence to pray to you about what I need! In Jesus' name, amen.

Week 5 • Day 3

Make Your Own Ice Cream

God protected the Israelites from the plagues. While the Egyptians had burning sores, the Israelites were cool and clean. How do you cool down when you are hot? A great way is to eat ice cream! If you make more than one bag, you can share extra ice cream with others.

What You'll Need

- 2 resealable plastic freezer bags: one gallon-sized, one quart-sized
- large bowl
- ½ cup half-and-half
- ice
- ½ cup rock salt or ice-cream salt
- ½ teaspoon vanilla extract
- 1 tablespoon of sugar
- **Optional:** gloves or hand towel

What You'll Do

1. Fill the gallon-sized bag about halfway with ice.

2. Pour in the salt.

3. Set the bag in the bowl.

4. In the quart-sized bag, pour in the half-and-half, sugar, and vanilla. Zip it shut.

5. Set the quart-sized bag into the gallon-sized bag.

6. Now move ice around so that the ice surrounds the quart-sized bag.

7. Press out the air from the gallon-sized bag, and zip it shut.

8. Now shake, move, jiggle, smoosh, and roll the bags. You want to get the cold from the ice transferred into liquid to make it ice cream.

9. After at least five minutes, check the ice cream to see if it is ready. Keep shaking and moving it until it is fully frozen.

Optional

If your hands are freezing, wear gloves. Or lay your bag in a hand towel. Grab the ends of the towel to make a sling for your bag.

Week 5 • Day 4

Facing Fears

Talking about facing our fears and having courage and boldness sounds great, doesn't it! But let's talk about the real things that happen every day; bullies, mean teachers, accidents, friends who turn out not to be friends, people who lie about us. How do we have courage and face those scary situations?

Here are some steps, courtesy of Jesus himself! *Read Hebrews 12:1–2 to begin looking at those steps.*

- First, we know we are right where we are supposed to be. *Read Ephesians 2:10 to remember who planned this!* God planned the things you are doing now long ago! He knows right where you are and what you need.

- Second, we fix our eyes on Jesus. How do we do that? When we start to worry, we tell that worry to him every time. You may have to pray every five minutes, but do it! Jesus knows every twist and turn of your life. He's also the one who makes us strong to run it well! That's why we can trust him to help us!

- Third, we remember the troubles he faced—he endured the cross, and he said, "I'll take the shame. It's no big deal, because I see the joy ahead of me— the joy of having my loved ones in my kingdom with me! That is well worth this suffering."

- Fourth, Jesus is now at God's right hand, interceding for us, talking to the Father about us! He loves us and he's on our side! *Read John 16:33 to see what Jesus told us.*

Yes, there will be trouble, but we can have peace. Jesus has overcome all that the world can use to try to scare us! We're on the winning side because our Savior has overcome.

Because of that, always remember that:

- You are where you are meant to be.
- Jesus has already run this race and you can trust him to coach and help you.
- Jesus loves you so much that even dying on the cross was not a big deal compared to how much he loves you.
- Jesus is in Heaven praying for you, talking to God his Father about you! He is the overcomer and he is on your side!

Your Turn

Think of a recent situation you heard about—a tornado, a storm, a hurricane, a big accident—and imagine you're writing a "courage note" to a kid your age who might have been in that situation. Use each of the "remember" statements on the previous page.

Remember

Remember

Remember

Remember

Remember

Week 5 • Day 5

Courage Rocks

When life becomes scary, we need to trust in God to be our foundation. He is immovable like a rock and he will encourage and comfort us. Today, use some rocks to remind yourself and others of how much God cares about you!

What You'll Need

- smooth rocks (like river rocks)
- permanent markers or paint pens
- **Optional:** acrylic paints, paintbrushes, cup of water (if you use acrylic paints)

What You'll Do

1. Think of words or pictures you can put on one side of the stone that would help you or anyone remember that God cares about you.

2. You can draw a smiling face on one side—simple! Or you can write a word or two from a Bible verse.

3. **Optional:** To make painted stones, paint as desired and let them dry before adding words with markers or white-out pen. (Painting words is much harder than writing them!)

When you have finished your stones, it's time for the fun part! You might keep a stone for yourself, but think of some good places to put the rest of them—maybe in the garden around your house (but not where a small person might swallow one!).

- You can give them to people you know.
- You can take some to a local park.
- Set them where people will find them, with the plain side up. When someone picks up the stone and turns it over, they'll have an encouraging moment!

Week 5 • Day 6

Reframing Charades

When we have a problem, we might hear others talk about "reframing" the problem. That is like turning the problem different ways to see how it can look different. Other people say it's helpful to "flip the script"—to look at the problem from an opposite way to notice possible good things that might come from it. It's a good thing to practice.

Play this charades game with your family. You'll be amazed at the different ways you come up with to think about problems!

What You'll Need

- Index cards
- Pencil or pen

What You'll Do

1. Gather everyone together. Brainstorm some situations that might worry a kid your age: getting picked last for the team, breaking your arm, losing your library book, wrecking your bike, catching a cold, etc.

2. On each card, write one of the hard situations. Include situations that have really happened, too!

3. Shuffle the cards.

4. Give a card to each family member (or a pair, if one person is very young).

5. First player acts out the situation on the card for the others to guess.

6. Everyone thinks of at least ONE good thing that might come from that situation.

7. Second player repeats step 5, but the family must now think of TWO good things that might come from that situation. Keep going, increasing the number of good things or unexpected happy results that might come from each situation!

Prayer

Lord, thank you for always watching over us, even when things feel scary. Remind us that you are always in control. Help us to trust in you always. In Jesus' name, amen.

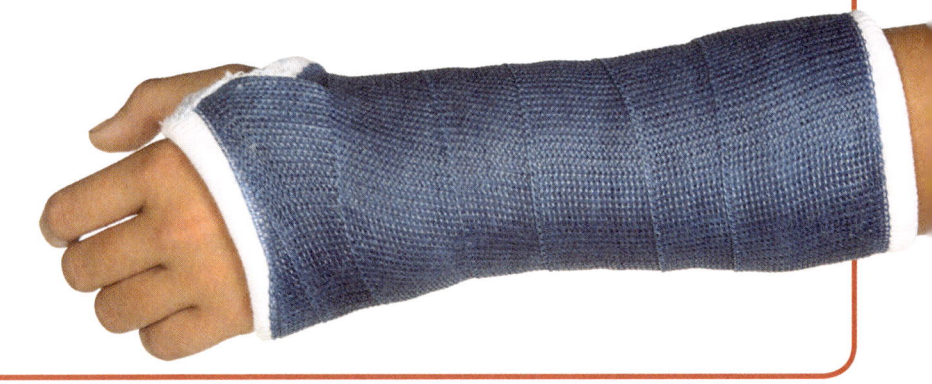

Week 6 • Day 1

Saved by God

God so loved the world that he gave his one and only Son. Anyone who believes in him will not die but will have eternal life.

JOHN 3:16 (NIrV)

There is salvation in no one else! God has given no other name under heaven by which we must be saved.

ACTS 4:12

First and Last
EXODUS 11:1-12:32; MARK 14:34-15:41; JOHN 14:12-14

Surprising Similarities

First and the Last Passover!

- The first Passover was the very last plague that God sent to Egypt. This plague was the worst of them all—death to the first-born child. Every Israelite family killed a lamb and painted its blood over the doorposts of the house. The blood was a sign for the angel of death to "pass over" the houses. The first-born children of the Israelites were saved by using the blood of a lamb.

- John the Baptist called Jesus "the Lamb of God who takes away the sin of the world" (John 1:29). Jesus is called the "Passover Lamb" in Hebrews because he is the perfect, sinless, one and only Son of God. Jesus blood was spilled and he died during Passover. Hebrews also tells us that when Jesus died, it was the last Passover anyone ever needed, even though Jewish people still celebrate this holiday.

First and Last Example!

- Celebrating Passover every year for thousands of years trained the Israelites to look for the last Passover Lamb, Jesus.

- That is why calling Jesus the "Lamb of God" was very important to those who were listening to him!

First and the Last Lambs!

- Each Passover lamb died to spare the children from death. The lamb's blood protected them. The lamb died in their place.

- Jesus died as the final Passover Lamb so that all people could be spared from spiritual death—separation from God—forever.

The Bigger Story

In John 1:29, read what John called Jesus. John could have called Jesus the "strong hero" or the "lion of Israel." But John called Jesus God's Lamb who takes away the sin of the world! When John said this, the people listening knew just what he meant—they had celebrated Passover every year of their lives! To describe Jesus as the perfect Passover lamb was something very familiar.

Read 1 Corinthians 5:7 to see how Paul describes Jesus. Here Paul is talking about the Jewish Passover tradition of cleaning up every bit of yeast. This was a symbol of turning from sin. But Jesus is the Passover lamb who is the "once and for all" sacrifice for sin.

Read Hebrews 9:11–12 to see the difference in Jesus' sacrifice. Jesus didn't bring animal blood to pay for our sin—he gave his own blood. He gave up his life so we could be saved from sin and become part of God's kingdom and family! Being saved from slavery in Egypt was amazing. But being saved from sin forever? That's far greater.

What's That Mean to Me?

Because Jesus made the sacrifice of his own blood, there is no need to ever make another sacrifice. Remember when Jesus said, "It is finished!" on the cross (John 19:30)? He meant it! In Acts 10, Peter told Cornelius, a Roman who wanted to know God, that everyone who believes in Jesus receives forgiveness of sins. Paul tells us in Romans 4:5 that God declares us **righteous** because of our faith in Jesus. We are **justified** in his eyes—just as good as Jesus is. *Find 1 John 5:20 to read it for yourself! Wow!*

It's clear that when Jesus saved us, he did more than give us a "get out of Hell free" card. He gave us an amazing, abundant life of goodness and righteousness and joy—because he loves us that much! Paul even says that if God didn't spare Jesus, but gave him up for all of us, why wouldn't he freely give us everything else we need? After all, by giving us Jesus as our Savior, he has already proved that he loves us more than we could ever hope or imagine!

If you've joined God's family, if you're part of his kingdom—congratulations! There is nothing more important. There is nothing better. Because **eternal life** is life with Jesus that never ends— it just gets more amazing and wonderful!

Righteous
living in harmony with God's laws, pleasing God, because God sees you as in his Son Jesus

Just, justified
Declared righteous in God's eyes; "just-as-if-I'd" never sinned

Eternal life
Life that is "at its best" and grows within us to last forever in God's presence.

Week 6 • Day 2

Your Turn

In what way is Jesus like a lamb?

In what way is Jesus like a priest?

What shows you that you are part of God's family and kingdom?

Prayer

Draw something that reminds you of what you think eternal life looks like.

Dear Jesus, the Bible tells us that we have never seen, heard nor imagined what you have in store for us in Heaven. But I thank you that you love me so much that you made the final sacrifice for sin. I believe you are God's Son and the savior. Thank you for loving me forever! Amen.

Week 6 • Day 3

Passover

When God told the Israelites to kill the lamb for Passover, he also told them to celebrate and remember when God freed them from slavery in Egypt. Over time, some foods became a tradition; the foods were also a way to teach children the parts of the Exodus story.

This is a Seder plate. The foods you see in this picture are often used in Israel and around the world to remember Passover. Each food represents a different memory about that night.

- **Parsley (or celery or lettuce)** reminds us that at first, the Israelites flourished in Egypt. But when the locusts and hail came to Egypt, the land had no more green plants. People dip the parsley in salt water. This reminds us of the tears the Israelites cried in Egypt, asking God to free them from slavery.

- An **egg** represents new life.

- **Matzo** reminds us of the unleavened bread which the people ate at the first Passover, because there was no time to let the bread rise.

- **Horseradish** is bitter (and pungent!) It reminds us of the bitterness of slavery.

- The **bone** (sometimes a lamb shank or a chicken leg) reminds us of the lamb that was sacrificed to keep each Israelite family safe. (Most people also eat lamb at this meal.)

- **Haroset** is a mixture of chopped apples, honey and nuts. It reminds us of the mortar the slaves used between the bricks they made when they were slaves in Egypt. Haroset is by far the tastiest item on a *Seder* platter! Enjoy it with matzo as you thank God for his sweet salvation in Jesus, the final Passover lamb!

Haroset is made many different ways, but here is one you can try with your family.

Haroset Recipe

What You'll Need

- 1 large apple, cored and cut into pieces
- ½ cup raisins or dates
- ½ cup of walnuts
- cinnamon, a pinch
- salt, a pinch
- 2 tablespoons honey
- ¼ cup grape juice
- blender

What You'll Do

1. Put all ingredients (except the grape juice) into a blender or food processor.
2. Add grape juice a little at a time as you process the mixture.
3. Chop until fine, and enjoy!

Week 6 • Day 4

Giving My All

Sometimes, we can forget just how world-changing and important it is that Jesus died for our sins. Even though eternal life begins with him, there is more to following Jesus! It isn't just life that is forever; it also grows inside us in ways we can't even explain! As we grow, we begin to see that there is more for us to learn and understand. *Look at Romans 12:1. What does this verse call our bodies?*

Wait. What? Didn't we just say that Jesus made the final Passover sacrifice? Why are we supposed to be sacrifices, too? When we realize God's great mercy, when we look at all Jesus has done for us, what else can we do? Thanking him with our whole selves only makes sense!

What is the sacrifice Jesus made for us? Read Hebrews 2:9 to see. Jesus sacrificed his life, tasted death for everyone. But how can we be a living sacrifice? It sounds like it could be hard. Maybe we won't get to stay the way we are now.

The answer is yes. And who'd want to stay the same? Would you want to still be sitting in a crib, staring at the wall? No! Why? Because you have grown past that stage of life. It's the same in our life with Jesus. People in his kingdom family keep on growing. We start out little, but we don't stay there.

In Romans 12:1–2, Paul says that giving God all of ourselves is "truly the way to worship" God. And at the end of verse two, he says this is God's "pleasing and perfect" will for us. In both verses,

Paul uses a Greek word that means "**satisfying**." Think of it this way: Giving God all we are is the kind of worship that satisfies God. Then, we experience living in his will for us and that satisfies us!

> **Satisfying**
> meeting our deepest needs and desires

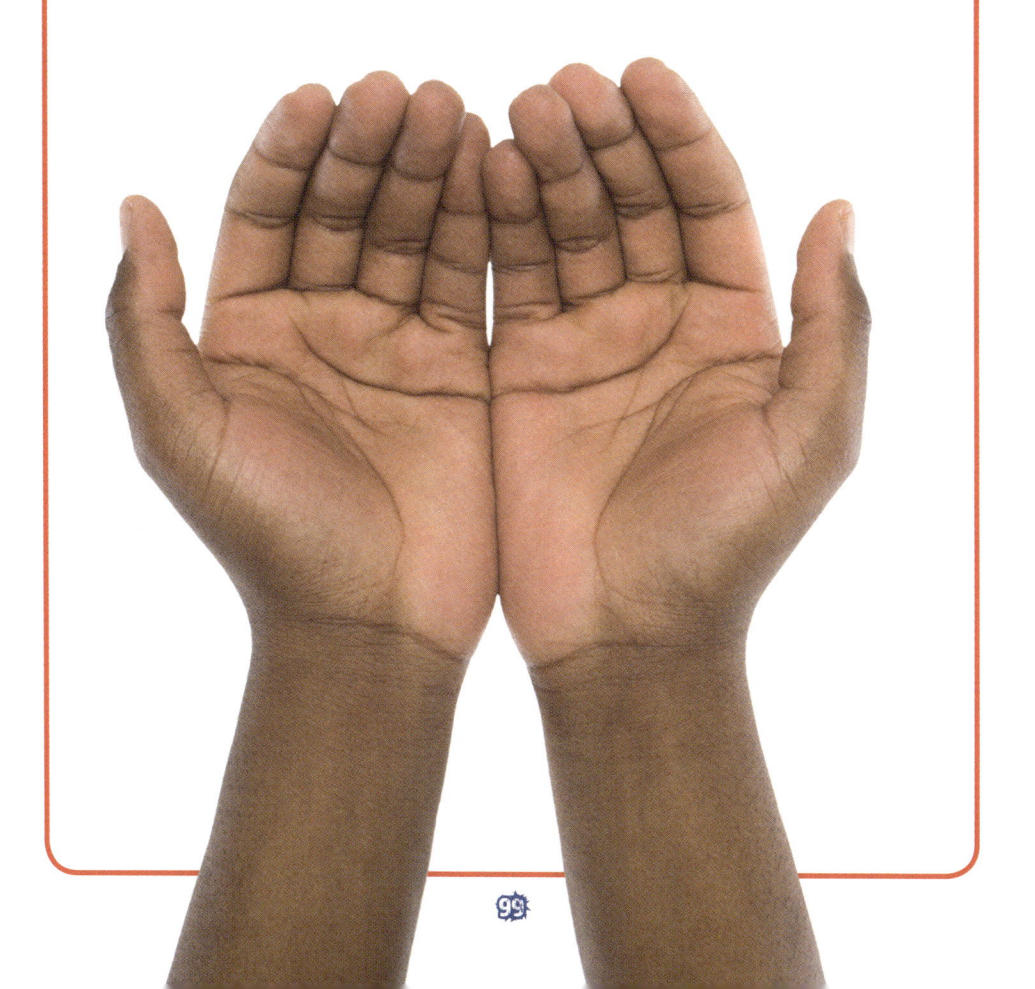

Your Turn

What is one thing you would tell a friend about why you are glad to be living in God's family?

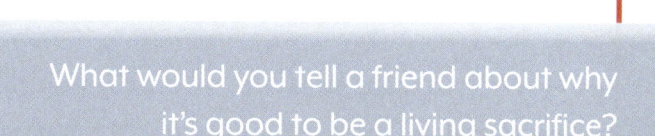

What would you tell a friend about why it's good to be a living sacrifice?

Week 6 • Day 5

All Clear

When Jesus died, he saved us from the punishment for our sins. Being forgiven makes us pure. If that is confusing, this experiment should clear it up. Try this with a grown-up family member. Watch to see what happens.

What You'll Need

- water
- clear, glass cup
- red food coloring
- spoon
- bleach (about ¼ cup)

> **Isaiah 1:18**
> Though your sins are like scarlet, I will make them as white as snow. Though they are red like crimson, I will make them as white as wool.

What You'll Do

1. Squeeze several squirts of red food coloring into the clear water. Stir it until all the water is red.

2. Now read Isaiah 1:18. What color does God say sin is?

3. Ask a grown-up to pour in the bleach, a little at a time. In between pours, stir the water.

> **1 John 1:7**
> If we are living in the light, as God is in the light, then we have fellowship with each other, and the blood of Jesus, his Son, cleanses us from all sin.

4. Watch. What happens to the red color?

5. Now read 1 John 1:7.

Jesus' blood takes away our sin—even better than the bleach takes away the red color from the water.

Prayer

Dear God, thank you that you never ask me to do anything alone. You are always with me. Thank you that you always give me what is the best thing for me, even on days I don't like it. I want to keep on growing in your family. Please help me to understand what it means to give you every part of my life—in every situation. In Jesus' name, amen.

Week 6 • Day 6

Dribble and Shoot

Jesus' goal on Earth was to save the world. Your goal in this game is to send your ball "around the world" (or around your circle). Play this game with your family to learn this week's verse.

What You'll Need

- Basketball
- Basketball goal (a hoop, a basket, or bucket—even a trash can)

What You'll Do

1. Stand in a circle with a basketball near the basketball goal.

2. Choose a person to be first.

3. Each person takes a turn to dribble the basketball. On each bounce, the person dribbling says one word of the Bible verse in order. (For example, "God," BOUNCE, "so," BOUNCE, "loved," BOUNCE, and so on.)

4. When the dribbler misses a word, the ball passes to the next person.

5. The next person tries to finish the verse, bouncing after every word.

6. Whoever finishes the verse shoots at the basket.

7. Play again. Can you dribble faster? Can you say the whole verse while you dribble?

8. Play the game until everyone can say the verse.

> **John 3:16 (NIrV)**
> God so loved the world that he gave his one and only Son. Anyone who believes in him will not die but will have eternal life.

Week 7 • Day 1

Freed by God

For he has rescued us from the kingdom of darkness and transferred us into the Kingdom of his dear Son.

COLOSSIANS 1:13

Jesus replied, "I tell you the truth, everyone who sins is a slave of sin. A slave is not a permanent member of the family, but a son is part of the family forever. So if the Son sets you free, you are truly free.

JOHN 8:34-36

True Freedom
EXODUS 12:33-42; ROMANS 6:18-23

Surprising Similarities

Escape Again!

- The Israelites originally went to Egypt to escape death by **famine.** After about 400 years, they left Egypt to escape slavery.

- As a baby, Jesus also went to Egypt to escape death. He left Egypt to live and obey God his Father—showing God's people he is the Savior.

> **Famine**
> a time when there is very little food to eat, usually because of not enough rain

Escape for all!

- The tenth plague killed the first-born children of the Egyptians, but the children of the Israelites were safe. Because of this plague, Pharaoh released the Israelites and all were able to go free.

- Jesus' death proved he has the power over the devil, who holds people in slavery through their fear of death (*see Hebrews 2:9–10*). Jesus made it possible for everyone who believes in him to escape slavery to sin (*Acts 13:39*).

As the morning dawned after Passover, Moses and the Israelites left Egypt. The Egyptians really wanted them to go! *Find out why by reading Exodus 12:33.* They were afraid they'd all die! And the Israelites didn't go out with just their own belongings. *Read Exodus 12:35–36 to see what else they took.* God made sure that the Israelites got their "back wages" for the years they had worked as slaves.

Suddenly, the Israelites were free—no more stomping on mud and straw to make bricks! No more lifting heavy bricks into place to make cities and pyramids. The Israelites were now free to worship God and follow him. They were free to work to help themselves and their own families.

Read Exodus 12:37 to find out how many Israelites left Egypt! With 600,000 men, that's well over half a million. Imagine that at least half of those men had wives and children. So, let's say that there were 300,000 who had at least a wife and two kids. Do the math! That's another 900,000! That's up to 1.5 million and there were probably more.

The Bigger Story

When Jesus came to earth, he came to give greater freedom to far more people than the million or so who were freed from slavery in Egypt! *What does the Bible call us in Romans 6:6?* Uh-oh! Who knew that we were slaves, too?

We are born into sin—that makes us slaves to our sinful nature.

Read Hebrews 2:14–15 to see what other kind of slavery Jesus frees us from. Beyond being stuck in slavery to sin, the devil has made all of us afraid of dying—another kind of slavery! But through Jesus' death and resurrection, we can be forgiven. That frees us from slavery to sin! Because Jesus didn't stay dead, but overcame death, he defeated the devil! The devil does not hold the power of death over people who believe in Jesus and are part of God's family. We don't have to be afraid of death, because by his resurrection, Jesus has already shown us that dying is nothing to fear. If we die here, we live with him forever!

What's That Mean to Me?

Think about it—guilt, shame and fear keep us feeling bound up. We can be slaves inside our own minds. Then we try to protect ourselves. We try to make ourselves look better than others. We look at others and silently tell ourselves what they aren't doing right. But because Jesus died and took our sin, we can be forgiven—and be free from fear, shame and guilt! If we're part of God's family, we never need to be afraid, ashamed or **guilty**, because Jesus has forgiven our sin! We never need to be afraid of death or the devil, because Jesus has proven he is stronger—he has overcome death and overcome the devil!

Guilt
knowing we've done wrong, broken the law, and may be punished

Shame
being upset and distressed because we are thinking or acting wrongly

God wants everyone to be this free! He has called us out of the power of darkness—that fear of death, slavery to **shame** and guilt—into Jesus' kingdom!

Week 7 • Day 2

Your Turn

What did God give the Israelites as they left Egypt?

What did Jesus come to do for every person?

What does God want to set us free from?

Prayer

Draw a picture that reminds you of how it makes you feel to know that once God forgives our sins, he doesn't remember them or hold them against us? Pray and thank God for his forgiveness and freedom while you draw!

Week 7 • Day 3

Set Free

Did you know there are still many people in the world who are slaves? Slaves are forced to work in a factory or a field or someone's house. They are not allowed to leave and go home to their families. What can a kid like you do about that?

Here's an Idea

With your family, look on the Internet. Find an organization that helps free people from slavery. Choose one of the organizations, and then select one of the following ways to raise money as a family. Donate the money to the organization you chose.

1. Everyone goes through their things to decide what is not needed. Gather them together and sell those things at a garage sale.

2. As a family, bake some goodies and then sell the goodies to friends.

3. Save your change. Set out a big jar by the front door. Every time a family member has coins, the coins go into the jar. In a few months, count the money.

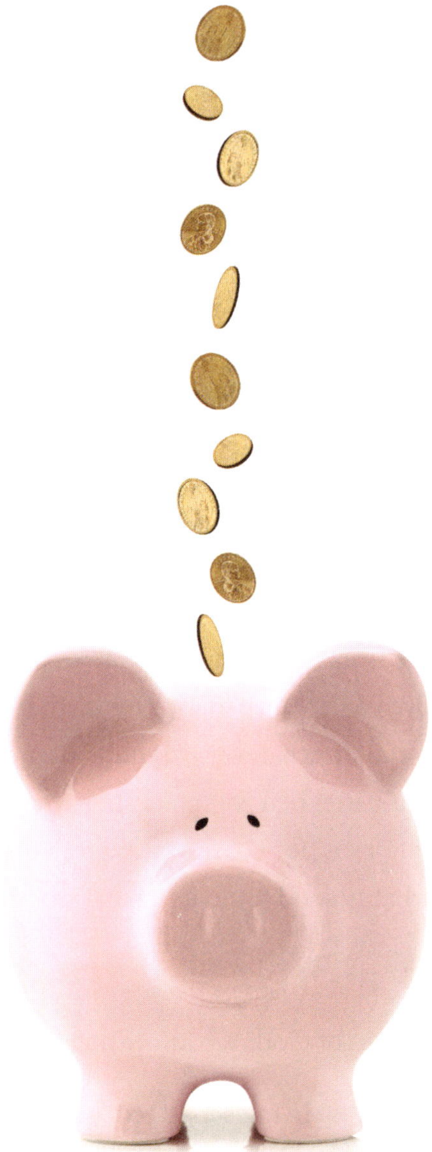

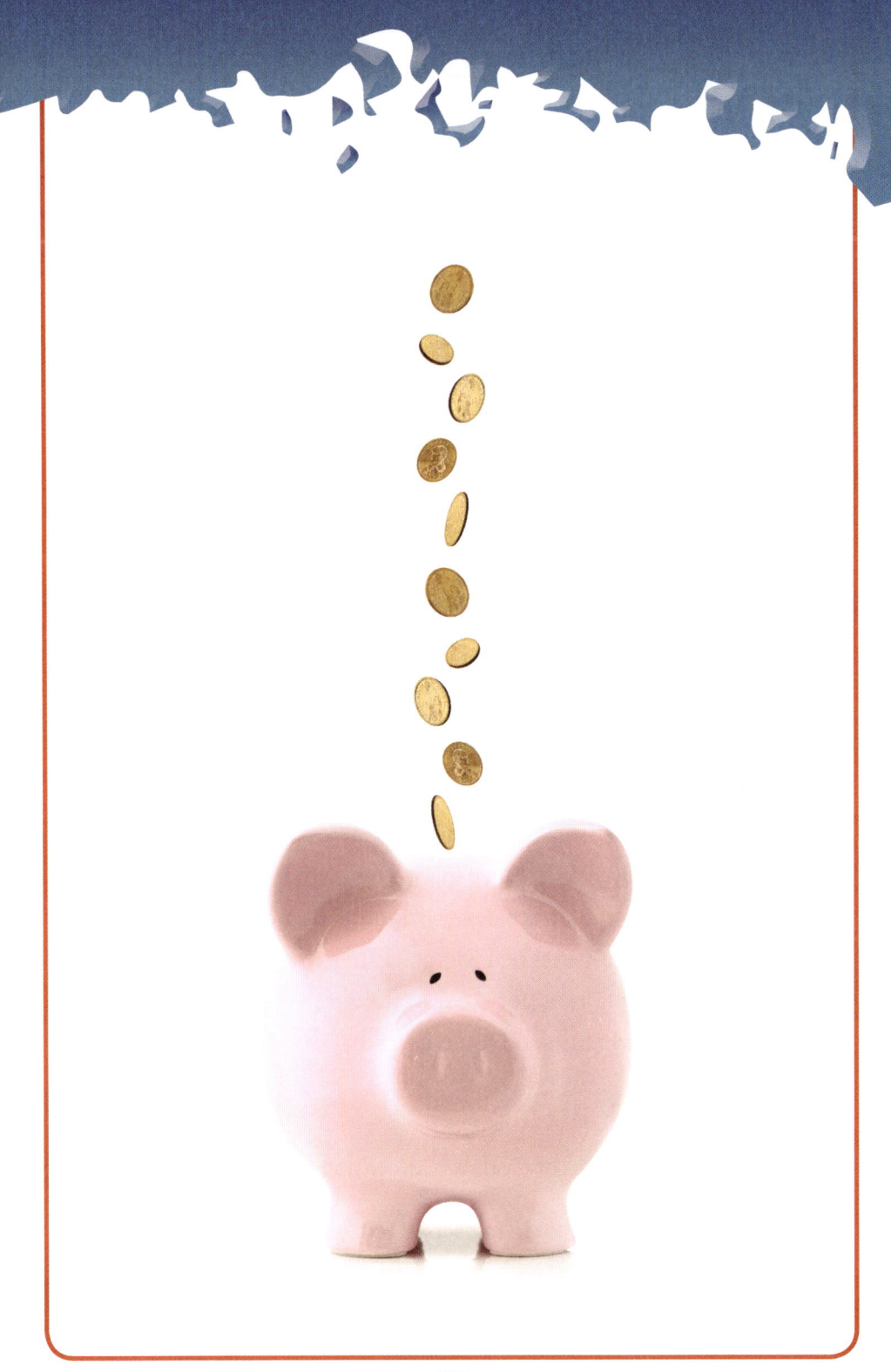

Week 7 • Day 4

Living in Freedom

Imagine how excited the Israelites were once they were out of Egypt! They must have felt like jumping and dancing—except that they were in a hurry to get as far away as they could!

Once we've been forgiven, we may feel like jumping and dancing, too! But after a while, that excitement wears off. How do we keep the excitement alive?

Before Jesus, the Jewish laws were meant to remind people of their freedom in God and that they were different from other nations. Obeying those laws made the Israelites "good." But the law couldn't make them free. It was "weak" because it relied on all that self-made "goodness"—or "the flesh"—which wasn't goodness at all.

We can only be free from God's grace and forgiveness. It is not something we can achieve on our own. Then, does freedom mean we can do whatever we want? Remember what Romans 12:1–2 told us? When we remember what God has done for us through Jesus, it makes us want to let him be the one who tells us what is good to do and what not to do!

What does it look like to *live in* freedom?

- We're not afraid of God. We know that he loves us.

- We're not afraid of being separated from God. *What can separate us from God's love? Read Romans 8:38–39 to find out.* We're safe from EVER being separated from his love.

- We're not bound to the old Jewish laws. *What replaced them? Read Hebrews 10:11–12 to find out.* We live under new promises. God has now written his law into our hearts! That means we're changed from the INSIDE, instead of hoping to please God by keeping laws on the OUTSIDE, the way the Israelites had done.

How do we *live out* our freedom?

- By living in ways that please God (remember that "satisfying" thing in Romans 12:1–2?).

- When we please him, we also live in ways that show others we belong to him.

- We forgive others in the same way Jesus forgave us—completely and freely. We don't hold a grudge or think it's OK to talk about them or demand justice.

When we live like that, we can easily do what 1 Peter 3:15 tells us. Read it to find out what it is! God has given us amazing, abundant lives in Jesus. He has set us free from sin, fear and unforgiveness. He makes us able to tell people both with our lives and with our words why we have the great hope he gives. That's a life of freedom!

Your Turn

What is one reason you feel free as a child of God?

In what part of your life do you still feel ashamed, guilty or fearful? Talk to God about those things. He loves you and wants you to be free of those things, too!

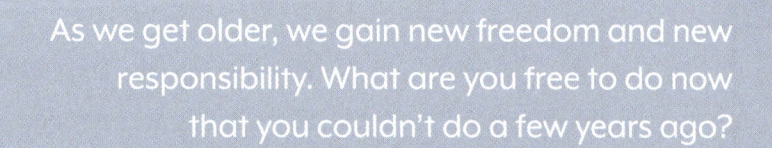

As we get older, we gain new freedom and new responsibility. What are you free to do now that you couldn't do a few years ago?

Week 7 • Day 5

Bound or Free?

To find out what Jesus said about becoming free, start at the star and go clockwise around the circle. Some letters are provided. On the lines below, print every other letter in order. When you get to the star, go around the circle the other way, writing every other letter.

E _ _ _ _ _ _ _ _ _ _ _ _ _ _ _ _ _ _
_ _ _ _ _ . . . _ _ _ _ _ S _ _ _ _ _ _ _ _ _
_ _ _ _ , _ _ _ _ _ _ _ _ _ _ _ _ _ _ _ _ _ _ _ .

Prayer

Dear God,

There are some things that make me ashamed. They are (*name them to God*)**.**

There are things that make me feel guilty. They are (*tell God what they are*)**.**

Some things that make me afraid of other people are (*tell God what they are*)**.**

I want to be free. Thank you that you are stronger than anything.

Thank you for forgiving me for everything.

In Jesus' name, amen.

Week 7 • Day 6

Prayer Chain

Today you get to make paper prayer chains because chains are often a symbol of slavery. As Christians, we are not chained to our sins. Our prayers and our dedication to God sets us free.

What You'll Need

- colored paper
- scissors
- tape

What You'll Do

1. Cut paper into strips. Each strip represents a family member. Feel free to include extended family or friends, too!

2. Write the family member's name on one side of the strip.

3. Write a prayer for them on the other side.

4. Take one strip and tape the ends together. It's your first chain.

5. Slip your next strip through the chain. Tape the ends of the strip together. Now the chains are linked.

6. Continue this all the way until all your chains are linked.

7. Hang the chain somewhere you look often. That way you'll remember to pray for your family often.

Week 8 • Day 1

Helped by God

For the word of God will never fail.

LUKE 1:37

Jesus looked at them intently and said, "Humanly speaking, it is impossible. But not with God. Everything is possible with God."

MARK 10:27

God Does the Impossible

EXODUS 14:5–14:31; MARK 4:35–5:42, 10:17–27; LUKE 1:33–37, 4:14–30

Surprising Similarities

Pursued by the enemy!

- The freed Israelites were pursued by angry Pharaoh and his army.
- Jesus was pursued by angry religious leaders.

Protected by God!

- God protected the Israelites in the form of a cloud. This way the Egyptians could not recapture them.
- When Jesus was pursued by an angry mob (Luke 4:14–30), God protected him. The crowd tried to throw him off a cliff, but Jesus escaped right through them.

Proven by God!

- God split the Red Sea so that the Israelites could escape from the Egyptians. He proved that he was with the Israelites and able to do the impossible.

- Jesus' many miracles proved God was with him. He turned water into wine. He healed people who had been sick for years. He brought dead people to life! All this was the work of God through Jesus.

After the Israelites left Egypt, Pharaoh realized he had made a HUGE mistake in letting all his slaves get away! Who would build the new Egyptian cities? Who would serve their food? Hundreds of angry Egyptian soldiers **pursued** the Israelites to enslave them!

> **Pursue**
> to follow someone and catch or attack them

The Israelites were trapped at the edge of the Red Sea. They had no boats and no way of getting across. Panicked and terrified, the people **wailed** to Moses, "Didn't we tell you to leave us alone? We'd be better off serving the Egyptians than dying in the desert!"

> **Wail**
> a cry of pain or anger

Read Exodus 14:13–14 to see what Moses said to these people. They didn't need to fear. God was with them and Moses was going to prove it! *Read what happened in Exodus 14:19–20.* The angel of God moved between the Israelites and the galloping army—and so the cloud moved from in *front* of the Israelites to *behind* them. Now the huge cloud stood between the Egyptians and the Israelites!

The cloud wasn't just a cloud, of course. It grew so dark over the Egyptians that they stopped because they couldn't see anything! But where the cloud faced the Israelites, it gave off light!

When Moses obeyed God's order and stretched out his hand over the Red Sea, God made the wind blow so hard all night that the water stood up—making a wall of water on either side. The Israelites walked across the sea while the Egyptians waited in the darkness of the cloud. Every single person and animal made it safely across!

After they were across, Moses lifted his rod and the sea came back together. And that stopped the pursuing army! God did the impossible for the Israelites.

The Bigger Story

The wind and water obeyed God to keep the Israelites safe from Pharaoh's army. We know Jesus made wind and water obey, too. *Look at Mark 4:35–5:42. Count the other miracles listed.*

- Jesus made the wind and water obey!
- He freed a man who had been tortured by evil spirits!
- He brought a dead girl back to life!
- He healed a woman who had been sick for *so* long, she thought she would *never* get well.

Jesus' miracles proved he is God's Son. His healing and feeding people showed them what God his Father is like.

When a rich man came to Jesus, he hoped to find out how he could have eternal life. *What did Jesus tell him? Read Matthew 19:16–30 to find out.* Which do you think the rich man loved more, following Jesus or having money? Jesus said that it was hard for a rich person to enter heaven. This really surprised his disciples, because they thought that rich people were blessed by God and must be on good terms with God. They had it backwards. Being rich did not mean the person was closer to God—this rich man had chosen his money *over* God!

What's That Mean to Me?

Jesus proved over and over that nothing is impossible for him. When we are part of his family, he gives us his Holy Spirit to be in us and to be with us. The Holy Spirit helps us to know what Jesus wants us to do so that we can obey him.

Read Hebrews 13:8 to see what it says about Jesus right now. God has never changed. Jesus has never changed. He still can do things that seem impossible for you. When you don't know what to do, pray. Ask him. Read God's Word to find out more about him. When you're in trouble, ask him to lead you! He will—and as you listen, obey!

Week 8 • Day 2

Your Turn

How does God help people when they are afraid?

How would you feel if God helped you in that way?

What would you tell him?

Prayer

Dear God, I'm drawing a picture of something that seems impossible to me. Let my drawing be a prayer.

Week 8 • Day 3

Stories of the Impossible

When Mary was told by an angel that she would be the mother of Jesus, that seemed impossible! But the angel told her how God would do this. The angel also told her that her very old cousin Elizabeth, who'd never had a child, was expecting a baby! Then the angel told her, "What God says will always come true" (Luke 1:37 NIrV). When God says it, it is done.

Hudson Taylor was one of the first missionaries to China. He learned how to follow Jesus and trust him for everything while living in that faraway place. He said, "There are three stages to every great work of God: first it is impossible, then it is difficult, then it is done." Sometimes we think a thing is impossible because we have never seen it. Today, take some time to talk with an older person.

What You'll Do

1. Ask this person to be your research buddy!

2. Think together about people who lived a hundred years ago.

   - What are things that we see every day that they could not imagine?

   - What things do we use daily that they thought were impossible?

3. Together, make a list of things people thought were impossible 100 years ago.

4. Then think about even twenty years ago. Make another list of things that were "impossible."

5. Invite your "research buddy" to tell you stories of things he or she thought were not possible when they were your age, too!

Week 8 • Day 4

Asking Always

Have you ever heard someone say, "Don't just stand there. Do something!"

The trouble is, if you don't know what to do, what should you do?

Lots of times, people think they are supposed to jump into action like some TV superhero. What do TV superheroes have that you don't? A script. They have it memorized. They know what is coming. They might *look* like they just thought of something, but we all know better!

Let's talk about what the best thing is to do in any situation! Just S. T. O. P.

- Stand still
- Think
- Observe
- Pray

When the Israelites were in a panic because the Egyptians were coming, what did Moses tell them? Read Exodus 14:13–14 to see. Notice that he did NOT tell them to run, to hide, to fight, to do something. He reminded them that God was with them. He told them that God was on their side and he would fight for them. Their job was to believe that God could do his job.

Now it's hard not to panic when everyone else is in a panic, but it is an ability you can practice and learn. When we take time to be still, to look around and then pray, we're in the perfect position to ask God for his wisdom. *What does James 1:5–6 say about wisdom?*

God promises to give us his wisdom when we ask. We don't need to second guess or freak out. Does that feel like you're not *doing* anything? It might, at first. But as a wise man once said, "We think that prayer begins the work, but prayer *is* the work."

When we have prayed and taken a moment to get God's wisdom, we have understanding. We have peace. We have the **expectancy** that God is going to do something to help us! That's the way he operates! He loves you, he will help you and he isn't going to leave you!

> **Expectancy**
> hoping that something positive will happen

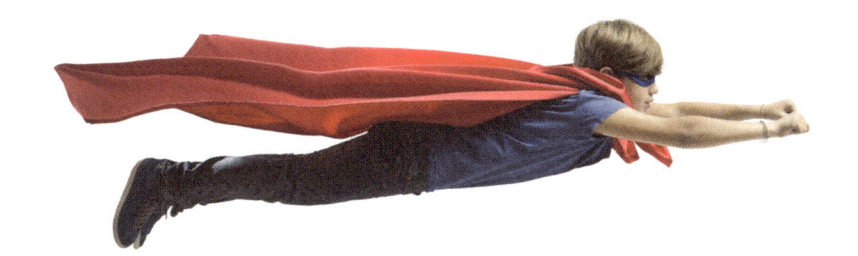

Your Turn

What did Moses tell the Israelites to do when they were in a panic?

Do you think God would ever fight for you? Why or why not?

What is one time you would really like to have God fight for you?

Week 8 • Day 5

Godly Guiding

We talk about how accurate and detailed mapping apps are, and how correct a Global Positioning System might be. But to find out just how detailed and how accurate God's Word is in knowing us and "positioning" us, fill in the missing vowels in this verse by using the symbols below.

A   E   I   O   U

Jesus looked at them intently and said, "Humanly speaking, it is impossible. But not with God. Everything is possible with God."

Mark 10:27

Answers on Page 221

Prayer

Dear God, sometimes I forget that the Bible is more than just stories. Help me to remember that it's the playbook—it tells me how you do things and who you are. Thank you for helping me remember to stop and to ask you in every situation. Thank you for giving me faith to trust you in every situation—even when everyone else is in a panic. In Jesus' name, amen.

Week 8 • Day 6

One-Handed Art

God sometimes does impossible things with human hands. Moses stretched out his rod to split the Red Sea. David used his hands to sling a stone at a giant's head. Jesus used his hands to heal the sick.

When we look at one of our hands, we see a hand. You can make many different art projects with the shape of your hand. Most of us have made a turkey shape out of our hands when we were in kindergarten. It's not exactly a turkey shape, but we can imagine a turkey, right?

What You'll Need

- paper
- markers

What You'll Do

1. Outline your hand on a few sheets of paper in the following shapes.

    - Fingers spread open
    - Fingers together
    - Some fingers bent
    - A fist
    - A fist with your thumb sticking out
    - A fist with your thumb and pinky sticking out.

2. Look at each of these shapes. What does it remind you of?

3. Turn the paper another way, does it remind you of something else? Let your imagination go—and see what "impossible" kinds of things you might see in your own hand's shape!

4. Add color, lines, whatever you like, to create something new from each hand shape.

Maybe one of your hand shapes will turn into a picture of one of those "impossible" things God made possible!

Week 9 • Day 1

Led by God

Trust the LORD with all your heart, do not depend on your own understanding.

PROVERBS 3:5

My sheep listen to my voice; I know them, and they follow me.

JOHN 10:27

God Guides

EXODUS 13:21-22; 15:22-27; JOHN 10:14-30

Surprising Similarities

Led by Light!

- The Israelites were led by a pillar of fire—God's presence in the darkness.

- Jesus said that he is the light of this dark world—those who follow him will not walk in the dark!

Led by Example!

- When Moses had a problem, he showed the Israelites what to do. He went right to God and prayed.

- When Jesus was tempted by the devil, he showed us what to do. He quoted memory verses to answer the devil and send him away.

Led by Promises!

- God had promised the Israelites that he would lead them to the land he had promised to give them. They had never seen it. They had no map and no description. They had to trust God to lead them to what he had promised.

- Jesus has promised us that we can hear his voice. He has promised to lead us by the Holy Spirit. He has promised us that one day, we will be with him where he is. We don't know *how* we'll get there. But we do know *who* will lead us and fulfill every promise he has made.

Without GPS or maps or anything else, the Israelites had no choice but to follow Moses. Moses didn't rely on his own ideas. He had to follow God. *Read Exodus 13:21–22 to find out the interesting way God lead his people.* Every day, the cloud of God's presence moved to guide the people.

The cloud was so HUGE that everyone could see and follow it—and, it gave them shade from the hot sun. At night, God sent a gigantic pillar of fire to guide them. Day and night, the Israelites had a clear and visible sign of God's love and guidance.

When they came to bitter water that they couldn't drink, Moses asked God what to do. When they needed food, Moses asked God what to do. Over and over, he didn't try to figure it out on his own. No, he asked God—and of course, God always had the right answer!

The Bigger Story

How is Jesus a greater leader than Moses? He is the Good Shepherd. What does a shepherd do? Everything his sheep need!

- He takes them to food and water
- He protects them from danger
- He applies medicine and cares for them

Read John 10:14–21 to find out what else the Good Shepherd did for his sheep. Notice that Jesus didn't die by mistake. He laid down his life. That means he died on the cross willingly. *That is deep sheep love.*

Jesus also talked about being a Good Shepherd when he was in the Temple. *Read John 10:22–30 to find out what Jesus told the people.* WOW! Jesus made it very clear that his miracles prove that he is the Son of God. His sheep hear his voice and follow him. He is one with God his Father. That means when we "sheep" hear his voice through the Bible or through another way, we can trust that he is really our Good Shepherd. He really wants the best for us.

What's That Mean to Me?

God's spirit was present in the cloud in Moses' time. God's spirit was in Jesus when he did miracles. Now, God's spirit is in you and in the Bible. When we read the Bible and ask God for guidance, it's better than using a GPS. Learn to sit quietly in his presence. Learn to dance in his presence. Learn to play fair or sing or draw or do chores in his presence. God is always with you. When you listen and obey him, you follow the best direction finder possible!

Week 9 • Day 2

Your Turn

What are some ways God led the Israelites?

If a friend asked you, "How can I know what to do? I feel unsure and confused!" What could you tell that friend? List at least three things you could say that would help your friend.

What are ways that Jesus leads us?

Prayer

Dear God, lots of times, I think I know what to do. Please help me to stop my thinking. Help me not to rely on my own understanding. I want to ask you first for help every time I need help. Thank you. In Jesus' name, amen.

Week 9 • Day 3

Listening Journal

Let's practice some ways to listen to Jesus' voice.

What You'll Need
- paper
- pencil

What You'll Do

1. Take time to get quiet. Put away the phone. Turn off everything that might distract you.

2. Listen. What do you hear? If you live in the city, maybe you hear traffic. If you live way out in the country, maybe you hear crickets.

3. List at least 5 things that you heard.

Now let's try a simple way to listen to what Jesus is saying. We call it the "P-C-E" method—for promise, command, and example. It's simple and it's kind of fun!

1. Make three columns on your page.

2. Write "P" at the top of one column. Write "C" at the top of the second column. Write "E" at the top of the third column.

> You may not fill up every column and that is OK. The important thing is to look at the passage in a different way.

3. Read John 10:7–30.

- What promises did Jesus make in this passage? Write them down in the "P" column. (There are a lot of these—try verses 9, 10, 16, 27, etc.)

- What did Jesus command us in this passage? Write that down in the "C" column. (See verse 18. Even Jesus had a command to follow!)

- What example did Jesus give in this passage? Write that in the "E" column. (in verses 7 and 11, what other names does he use? How are those examples? The way Jesus obeys the Father in verse 15 is an example, too.)

4. Read your answers aloud to yourself. That way, you listen to what Jesus is saying in this passage.

Try this with other passages and see what you learn by breaking a passage down in this way!

Week 9 • Day 4

Listen and Obey

Have you ever had a pet that just didn't listen? Maybe you've had a dog that wants to play fetch, but then he won't put down the ball so you can throw it again. What do you do? You keep saying, "Put down the ball!" If your dog doesn't obey, then you stop playing with him. Because for there to be a great fetch-and-throw relationship between you and your dog, the dog needs to listen and obey!

Read Deuteronomy 6:4–6 and find the word, "Listen." In Hebrew, the language that the Old Testament was written in, that word "listen" is pronounced, "sh-MA." It means more than just hearing like you'd listen to the TV. It means to listen **intently**, because you are about to obey what you hear. When God talks, when he guides us, we need to listen and be ready to obey what we hear. Like your dog, there isn't a good relationship with God if we want to listen but not to do what he says.

> **Intently**
> to do something with eager attention or focus

Often, we don't hear a big, long plan. God shows us what to do next or where to go. People sometimes complain that they want God to show them the whole plan of their lives. But God doesn't work that way. He doesn't present you with a blueprint and invite you to sign your name to say you approve!

Instead, God often gives us just what we need to do the next thing, to take the next step. Why? Because he wants you and me to "trust in the LORD with all your heart; [and] do not depend on your own understanding" (Proverbs 3:5). God says that when we look to him then we can easily submit to him and say, "You are God and I am not! I want to do what you want me to do."

And the result? Best. Guidance. Ever. Because he knows where you need to go. He will make the path clear for you so that you're not confused or panicked! You can totally trust and fully obey God's plan.

Your Turn

If you pick up a phone call from a blocked number, how can you tell who is calling? If it's your mom, how do you know it's her, without her saying, "This is mom"?

How is hearing Jesus' voice like that phone call from mom?

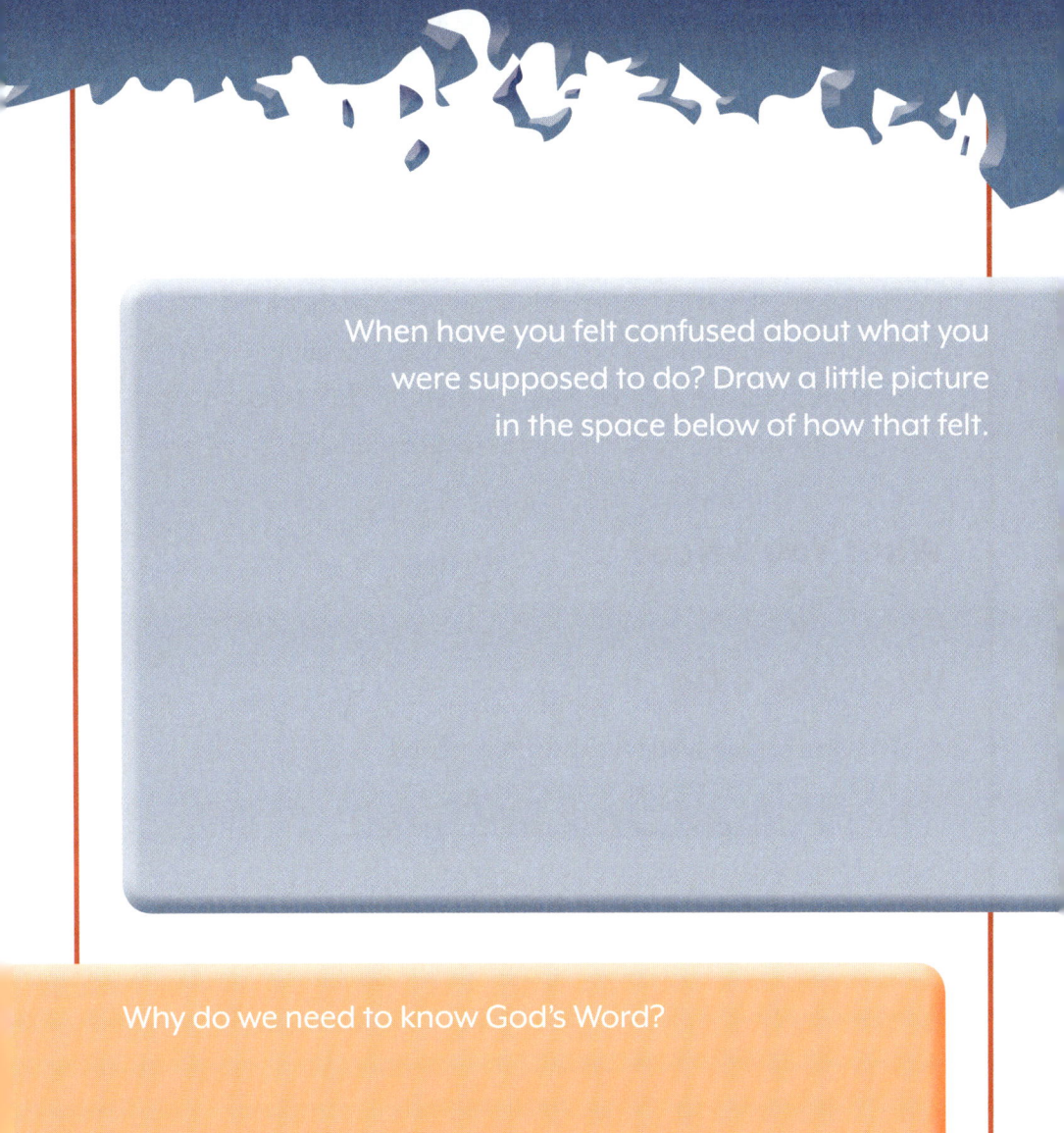

When have you felt confused about what you were supposed to do? Draw a little picture in the space below of how that felt.

Why do we need to know God's Word?

Week 9 • Day 5

Do You Draw What I Draw?

Everyone sees the world differently. How we view the world affects our imaginations. Two people can hear the same description and have different ideas in their heads. Do this activity with your friends or family to see for yourself.

What You'll Need
- paper
- markers

What You'll Do

1. One person reads the directions aloud.

2. Everyone draws as the directions are read.

3. After all directions are read and everyone has drawn, show each other your papers.

Directions

1. Draw a circle in the middle of the page.

2. Draw some wiggly lines.

3. Draw a circle smaller than the first one.

4. Draw three triangles near the corner of the page.

5. Draw a straight line.

6. Draw two squares near the circle.

7. Draw the biggest triangle you can.

8. Draw a cat in the triangle.

9. Draw a tree.

10. Draw a sun.

Are they all the same? No—but you all followed directions!

Prayer

Dear God, Thank you that you always hear me. Thank you that I can trust you to answer. Please help me to be ready to do what you tell me in your Word and by your Holy Spirit, even if it is just one small act. In Jesus' name, amen.

Week 9 • Day 6

With All Your Heart Comics

Proverbs 3:5 tells us to trust in the Lord with all our hearts and to not depend on our own understanding.

What You'll Need

- paper
- markers

What You'll Do

1. Choose one of the scenarios provided or come up with your own.

2. Draw a comic strip about your reactions. What would it look like to trust in the Lord with all your heart in that situation?

Scenario 1: School Bus on the Way to School

Beautiful, curly-haired Alia taps your shoulder from the seat behind. You turn and she flashes you her winning grin. "Can I see your homework assignment on the Rainforest monkeys?" You nod, but before you hand it to her, you ask, "Why do you want to read it?" Alia twirls her hair. "Oh I just forgot mine at home and I don't want to get a bad grade. I wanted to get some ideas from your paper so I can rewrite mine now. I just knew you'd be ok with it because you wouldn't want me to get a bad grade either."

- **What do you say? What do you do?**

Scenario 2: Cafeteria at lunch

Max throws a paper airplane at you from a different lunch table. You open it and discover a drawing of your teacher with fangs, red eyes, and horns. At the top of the drawing it says "Pass it on." You look back at Max who is laughing. Some kids around you lean in to see the picture. They also laugh.

- **If you don't laugh, what will your friends say? What will you say? Do?**

Scenario 3: Classroom

"Sam and Tucker you'll be working together for the solar system project," Ms. Jackson announced. Sam groaned. Tucker was slouched in his chair, half asleep, and barely heard the news. Sam rolled his eyes. *How am I going to get a good grade when I have to work with him? He doesn't care about anything and he definitely doesn't care about grades.*

- **What do you do? Say?**

Week 10 • Day 1

Asking God

Seek the Kingdom of God above all else, and live righteously, and he will give you everything you need.

MATTHEW 6:33

It is impossible to please God without faith. Anyone who wants to come to him must believe that God exists and that he rewards those who sincerely seek him.

HEBREWS 11:6

God Provides
EXODUS 16:1–17:7; JOHN 6

Surprising Similarities

Water to Live!

- When the thirsty Israelites were wandering in the desert, God gave them water out of a rock.

- Jesus said, "Anyone who is thirsty may come to me," because he is the source of living water (John 7:37).

Food to Live!

- God sent manna (bread from heaven) and quail to feed the Israelites.

- Jesus turned five loaves of bread and two fish into enough food to feed thousands. Jesus said "I am the living bread that came down from heaven" (John 6:51).

Prayer to Live!

- Moses prayed and asked God to feed the Israelites so they wouldn't starve in the desert; God sent more manna and quail than the people could eat!

- Jesus prayed over a boy's small lunch and fed thousands of people. They had twelve baskets of leftovers.

Moses knew that God had the answer to every need the Israelites had. God was never surprised. He loved them and had promised to provide for them. God always keeps his promises. During the many years the Israelites lived in the desert, God provided them with food. Even their clothes and sandals never wore out!

The Bigger Story

Jesus preached for a long time and soon everyone got hungry! *Read John 6:5–7 to see what Jesus asked his friends. What did Philip say about feeding these people?* The disciples didn't know what to do!

Andrew, another disciple, brought a boy to Jesus who had five pita rounds and a couple of fish! "What good will this do among so many people?" he asked.

Jesus knew what to do. He gave thanks to God his Father for the bread and the fish, and began to break it into pieces. Soon, the disciples were running with their big baskets of fish and bread to one group, then another. Just like the time God sent quail to the Israelites, everyone ate until they were full. And there was plenty left over!

Just as God his Father was not surprised by how the Israelites acted in the desert, Jesus was not surprised by what these people wanted to do. *Read what they wanted to do in John 6:14–15.* Why do you think Jesus got out of there and went away to pray?

The next day, some of the same people found Jesus again. *Read what Jesus said about bread in John 6:25–26.* What do you think spiritual bread is? Jesus wanted them to know God, to become part of God's kingdom through believing in him.

What did Jesus call himself? Read John 6:48–50 to find out. Jesus was going to give his body to die for the sin of the world, in the same way God the Father gave the manna to keep the Israelites alive in the desert. Jesus said that anyone who believed in him would live with him forever. This is the spiritual "bread" that Jesus IS—and the "bread of life" he gives.

So, Jesus came not only to feed but also to satisfy the people's spiritual need to know God and be part of his kingdom!

What's That Mean to Me?

To find out what God will do for you, read Philippians 4:19 aloud from your Bible. This promises us that our needs will be met through Jesus. This does not mean we won't ever feel hungry or thirsty. It doesn't mean that we get anything we want. It means that Jesus will always give us what we need. Loving God is the main thing. And he'll take care of the other things.

God will take care of us in every way. That is even a greater miracle than getting water from a rock or mystery bread in the desert. All we need to do is to ask and believe.

Week 10 • Day 2

Your Turn

How did God take care of the Israelites in the desert?

What ways did Jesus tell the people who were fed that he would care for them?

What can we trust God to do for us when we need something?

Prayer

Dear God, what I'm drawing shows something I believe I need. Thank you for giving me what I need. And if I don't need it, please give me wisdom to know that, too. In Jesus' name, amen.

Week 10 • Day 3

Food Drive

Good takes very good care of our needs. That includes food, housing, clothes, and more. Because he gives us a lot, we can share with others. Today, start a food sharing project. Invite your friends and neighbors to help.

What You'll Do

1. Make a flyer. On a sheet of paper, write a big headline: "FOOD DRIVE."

2. Under that, write: "Please put out bags of canned goods or dried food on (date). I will pick up the food on that day. We will donate the food to (Choose a location. Ask your parents to help you choose.)."

3. Post your flyers in your neighborhood or give them to your neighbors.

4. On the day of the food drive, take a wagon and go house to house. Pick up bags of food in your wagon.

5. At the end of your pickup, go with your parents to the place you promised to give the food.

After you deliver the food, take a photo. Use the photo on your next flyer. Also, don't limit yourself to just food. One month, you could ask for clothes donations instead. Then do toy donations the next month. If you ask people to donate on the same day every month (for instance, the first Saturday), they will get used to it.

Week 10 • Day 4

Trusting Completely

Sometimes, we don't know what we need. That's why God invites us to ask him for wisdom—we can ask him to help us know what we need. Can you quote James 1:5? It's a good one to remember!

Sometimes, we want what we don't need. *Read Romans 8:28 to see what God says about what he sends us.* God promises to work things for our good. He knows what is best for us! So when we don't get a "yes" answer to a prayer, we can trust God and know he has something better for us.

Read Hebrews 11:4 to find out what it says about faith—trusting God. Sometimes, we are around a lot of people who say great words about God and we feel like we can trust God completely! Other times, when we are bothered by life, it's easy to forget to trust God. Our first reaction is to think, "I can fix this problem. I'll take care of it. I can't trust anyone else to do it." But that is exactly what God does NOT want us to do.

See the bird in the photo? It's being fed by a human. Now that bird could be on the ground, finding whatever was there, taking care of eating on its own. But because that bird trusts the human feeding it, it's eating on a whole different level. It's feasting on seeds and other good things it would not usually find on the ground!

We're kind of like that. We think we can fix our problems ourselves. We can go our own way. We can ignore God if we think he is not doing what WE think he should do (and who do we think we are then?). But if we will trust God completely, if we will believe that he loves us, we'll discover that many amazing good things will come to us.

Like eating Jesus' "bread of life," we discover blessings and benefits that would never come to us when we go it alone! When trusting isn't easy, remember this photo. Trust will take us places that relying on ourselves never could.

Your Turn

What does God promise in James 1:5 that he will give us? What do we have to do?

What does God promise in Matthew 6:33 that he will give us? What do we have to do?

What does God promise in Hebrews 11:6 that he will give us? What do we have to do?

Week 10 • Day 5

Archimedes' Screw

When the Israelites needed water, Moses hit a rock—and it poured out. Think you can get water from a bowl into a glass WITHOUT pouring it out?

Here's a dramatic and ancient way to get water from one place to another! Archimedes was a mathematician, physicist, and inventor in ancient Greece. He realized that a screw is a ramp that is wrapped around a cone or rod. He thought up this way to move water by pushing it up the ramp from one place to another!

What You'll Need

- bowl, half full of water
- food coloring
- drinking glass
- clear packing tape
- can or length of wide PVC pipe
- clear plastic tubing, quarter inch (available at home supply stores)

What You'll Do

1. Squirt a little food coloring into the water in the bowl so you can easily see the water. Set it aside while you make the screw.

2. Use the clear tape to attach the plastic tubing to the can/pipe. Start by taping one end of the tube at the bottom edge of the can/pipe. Then work your way up in a spiral, taping the tube as you go.

3. When you get to the top, cut off any excess tubing, so about an inch extends.

4. Now set the bottom end of the screw at an angle into the bowl of water.

5. Set the glass where it can catch the water.

6. Now turn the screw!

What happens? Every time the screw "comes up for air" it gulps a bubble that pushes the water on ahead of it. See if you can get most of the water moved. Look online to see how many big machines use the principle of Archimedes' Screw.

Prayer

Dear God, Thank you that faith is a gift from you, and that you can help me to trust you more. I want to trust you even when things don't look good to me. In Jesus' name, amen.

Week 10 • Day 6

Wall of Words

This week you learned to seek the Kingdom of God before all else. Kingdoms are usually guarded by walls for protection. There are some very important words hidden here, but you're going to have to get them out of the wall! To dig out the words you need to:

1. Cross out every color name.
2. Cross out every fruit name.
3. Cross out every kind of transportation.
4. Cross out every name of a school subject.

Now read from left to right, top to bottom, to fill in the blanks!

It is _____ to _____

_____ without _____. Anyone _____

wants to _____ to him _____

_____ that God _____ and that he

_____ those who sincerely _____ him.

Hebrews 11:6

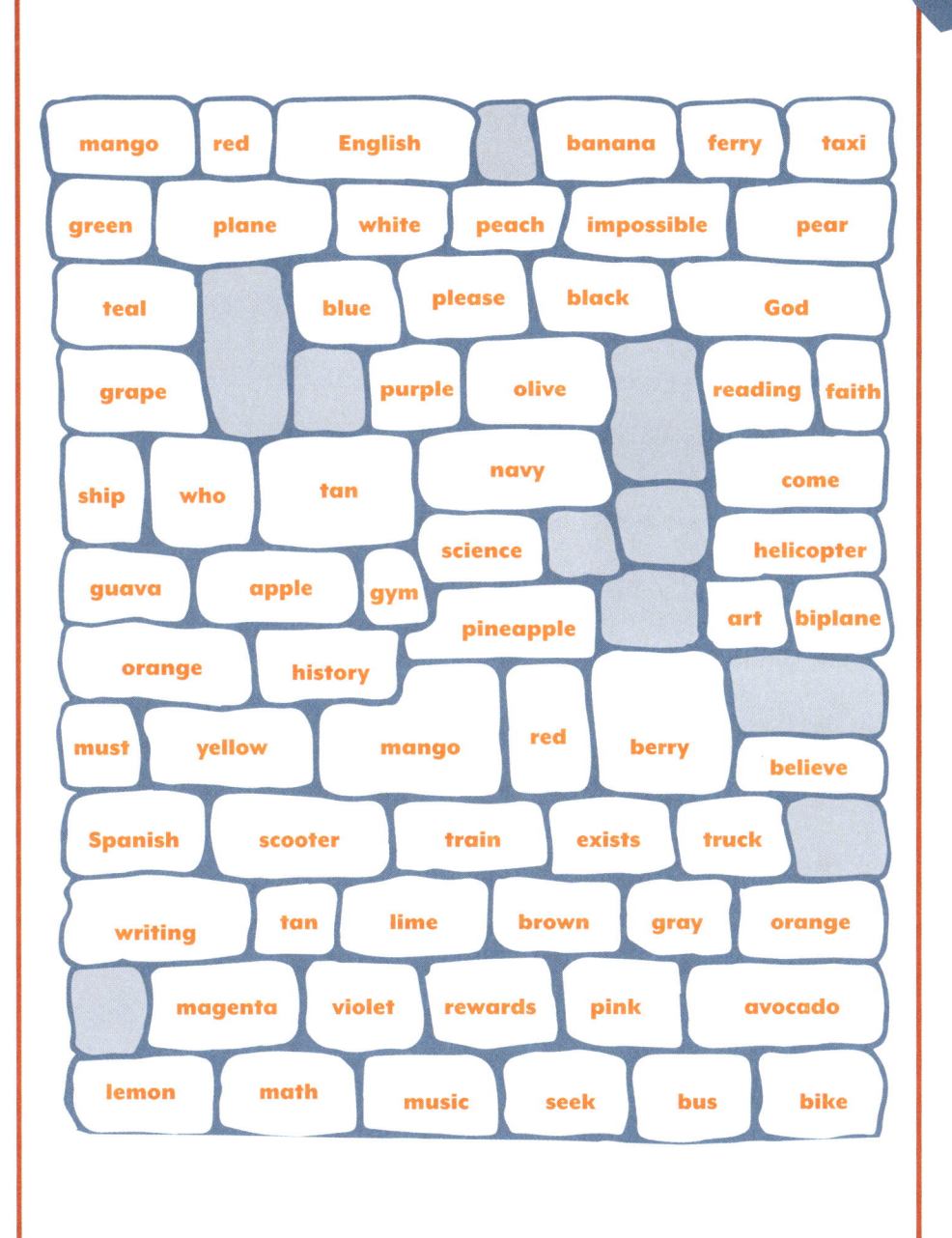

mango	red	English		banana	ferry	taxi
green	plane	white	peach	impossible		pear
teal		blue	please	black		God
grape		purple	olive		reading	faith
ship	who	tan	navy			come
			science			helicopter
guava	apple	gym	pineapple		art	biplane
orange	history					
must	yellow	mango	red	berry		believe
Spanish	scooter	train	exists	truck		
writing	tan	lime	brown	gray	orange
	magenta	violet	rewards	pink	avocado
lemon	math	music	seek	bus	bike

Answers on Page 221

Bonus: Respond-O-Meter

Jesus told us that loving others is the way we fulfill the "law" of the ten commandments. When we love God and love others, we will do what the law says, not because we have to, but because we can't imagine doing anything else! But how do we live that out?

Here's a fun way to help you respond to people in love, in every situation

What You'll Need

- 2 sheets of poster board
- Plate (or something else round, like an ice cream lid)
- Fine-tip marker
- Scissors
- Ruler
- Paper fastener

What You'll Do

1. Lay both poster boards flat on table and place the plate on top of one.

2. Draw around the plate to make a circle on each sheet of poster board.

3. Cut out each circle.

4. Use the ruler to draw lines on ONE circle to make 8 triangles (like pieces of pie).

5. In each of the pie shapes, write something kind or loving you might say to another person when they are mean or angry. Write in each of the shapes.

6. On the second circle, draw one triangle (one piece of pie) and cut it out.

7. Put the second circle on top of the first.

8. Use the paper fastener to make a hole in the center of both circles. Push it through and fold back the pieces on the back side so it will spin.

Now have some fun with your family and friends. Invite them to describe a situation in which another person might be mean or angry or unkind. Have them spin the Respond-O-Meter. Read the answer aloud and then talk about whether that response might help in that situation. Then invite them to tell other ways they might be a better way to respond.

Week 11 • Day 1

Loving God

Love the Lord your God with all your heart, all your soul, all your mind, and your strength. The second is equally important: Love your neighbor as yourself. No other commandment is greater than these.

MARK 12:30-31

Now I am giving you a new commandment: Love each other. Just as I have loved you, you should love each other.

JOHN 13:34

Perfect Commands
EXODUS 19:1-20:21; MATTHEW 22:34-40

Surprising Similarities

Giving the Law and Giving the Power to Obey It!

- God gave Moses the Ten Commandments on Mount Sinai fifty days after the Israelites left Egypt. Today, Jews celebrate the Feast of Weeks or the Feast of First Fruits to remember this event. (In Greek, "fifty days" is "Pentecost.")

- Fifty days after Jesus' death and resurrection God sent the Holy Spirit at Pentecost. Jesus had fulfilled the law. So, in the new **covenant,** God sent us the power to obey everything people could not obey before!

The First and Last Mediators!

- Moses was the first **mediator** of God's covenant with the Israelites.

- Jesus is the final mediator of God's covenant with all people.

The Big Noises!

- When God made the old covenant at Sinai there was darkness, earthquakes, and a loud trumpet blast.

- When Jesus died, God made a new covenant. Again, there was darkness, earthquakes, and the loud voice of Jesus who cried out, "It is finished!"

> **Covenant**
> a set of promises between two people or groups. Our faith is based on the covenants God made with Abraham, Moses, and David

> **Mediator**
> a person who goes between two arguing people. They help them agree on something

When the Israelites came to Mount Sinai (SIGH-nyi), God was ready to make them his own special people. God gave them rules to live good lives. These rules (and there were more than the ten) were part of a promise, or covenant, God made with them.

Living by God's rules made the Israelites different from everyone else around them. *What did the Israelites say about this? Read it in Exodus 19:8.* They were sure they could follow all the rules. The deal was if the Israelites obeyed, God would protect them, do miracles, and forgive their sins.

The Bigger Story

The problem with the Israelites was that they broke their promise to God over and over again for 1500 years before Jesus came to earth. Jesus fulfilled every part of the law because he obeyed and trusted God his Father completely. He never broke a rule. Can you imagine that? Jesus' death and resurrection guarantees that what God promises in this new covenant will happen. And the good news is, we're part of the new covenant!

God says something very important about this new covenant. Read it in Hebrews 8:10.

If God *changes* us, if he writes his laws on our hearts and minds, then we never need to rely on our own strength to trust God. We can ask him for faith to trust him. We can ask him to help us obey!

Hebrews 9:15 says that Jesus "mediates a new covenant between God and people, so that all who are called can receive the eternal **inheritance** God has promised them." Part of God's family? Then you're free! You're forgiven! You're under a whole new covenant that will end with you receiving all that God promised!

> **Inherit/Inheritance**
> to get money or property because the previous owner died

What's That Mean to Me?

Read 1 Peter 2:9 to find things about God's family that are amazing! Does this sound like what God told the Israelites way back at Mt. Sinai? Peter says we are a kingdom of priests and a holy nation, just like God said about them!

What does it mean to be a priest and part of God's kingdom?

- We love people, especially when they are not easy to love.

- We pray for people, especially people who have been mean to us.

- We do good to all people, especially other people in God's kingdom—because Jesus gave us two levels of love.

> First: "Love the Lord your God with all your heart, all your soul, and all your mind, and all your strength" (Mark 12:30).

> Second: "Love your neighbor as yourself" (Mark 12:31).

Those two commands are so important that all the others come from it. When we obey those TWO commands, we obey all TEN commands God gave to Moses.

We're God's special people—but we didn't become those people by obeying his commands perfectly. You see, Jesus obeyed God perfectly! And he took the punishment we deserved for not always obeying. When we believe in Jesus, he makes us right with God.

Week 11 • Day 2

Your Turn

What did God say he would do for the Israelites if they obeyed him? How successful were they?

What did God call us in 2 Peter 2:9?

What do we have to do to keep our part of this covenant?

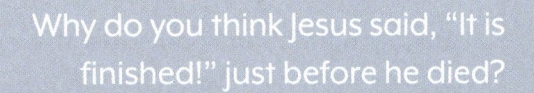

Why do you think Jesus said, "It is finished!" just before he died?

Prayer

Dear God,

You call me _____ and _____ .

You tell me I can ask you for _____ to trust you and for _____ to obey you. You did everything because you knew I couldn't do anything!

Thank you for making it possible for me to be part of your kingdom. It's amazing. In Jesus' name, amen.

Week 11 • Day 3

Commandment News Search

We often don't think about it, but the Ten Commandments are the foundation of our laws and a whole lot of our culture. So today, let's check out how the "big ten" play out in everyday life—by checking the newspaper!

What You'll Need

- A copy of the Ten Commandments (Exodus 20:1–17)
- Newspaper, either the paper kind or online
- The handy form on the other page

What You'll Do

1. Choose three articles based on their headlines.

2. Read the headline. Which commandment do you think is being broken?

3. Read part of the article. Which commandment applies to the situation described in the article?

You'll start to see why the "big ten" are a big deal!

Headline: _____

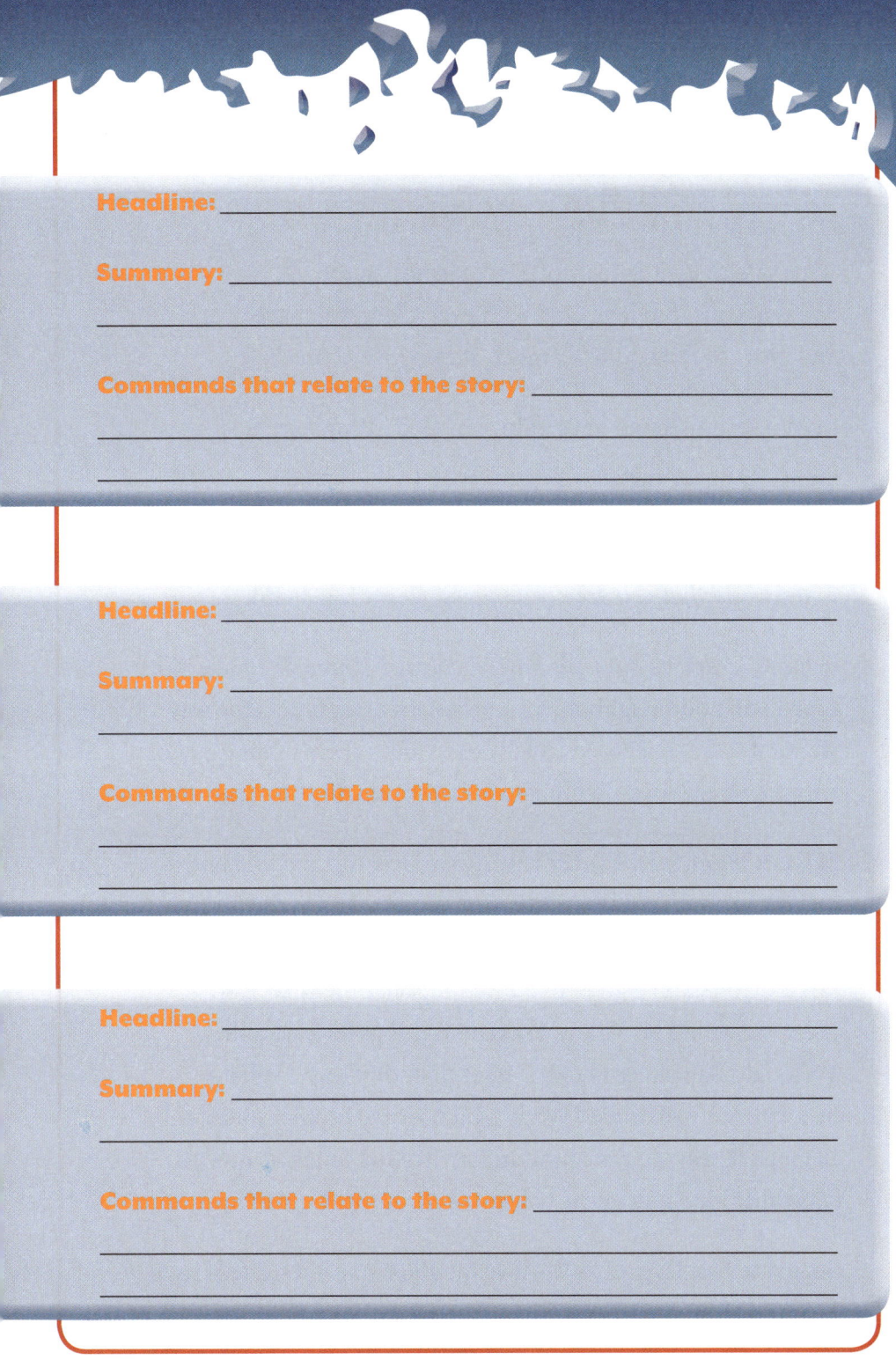

Summary: _____
_____

Commands that relate to the story: _____
_____
_____

Headline: _____

Summary: _____
_____

Commands that relate to the story: _____
_____
_____

Headline: _____

Summary: _____
_____

Commands that relate to the story: _____
_____
_____

Week 11 • Day 4

Living by Jesus' Law

Jesus said that all the law of Moses hangs on the commandment to love God with everything you have and love your neighbor as much as you love yourself.

But there is a second level of love in God's Kingdom. Just before Jesus died, he told his disciples, *"I am giving you a new commandment: Love each other. Just as I have loved you, you should love each other. Your love for one another will prove to the world that you are my disciples"* (John 13:34–35).

What kind of love did Jesus have? Look at 1 John 3:16 to see. More than loving our neighbor as ourselves, treating others the way we want to be treated, Jesus tells us to love others in his kingdom with sacrificial love—willing to lay down our lives for them.

What is the greatest kind of love? Read John 15:13 to find out. Of course, we're not Jesus. We may not be asked to die for our friends in God's family. But the point is that in God's kingdom family, God's Spirit gives us a love for each other that is so great, we would be willing to do hard things for each other. We would be willing to die. Rather than thinking, "What's best for me?" we think, "What is best for my brother or sister in God's family?" As we pray and invite God to tell us how to show that kind of love, he will also give us that kind of love!

So, in the first level of love—love for all people—Jesus tells us to love and treat every person just the way we would like to be treated.

That is one way we act as God's royal priests. That kind of love will get people's attention because true kindness is rare and surprising!

Then, we love the others in God's kingdom family even more than that—with the sacrificial kind of love like Jesus had for us. He loves us so much, he would do anything for us. And by the Holy Spirit, he makes us able to love like that. WOW!

We can always ask God to help us love him and love others with everything we have. He sent his Holy Spirit to help us keep Jesus' law of love—on the very day his people were celebrating giving the law of Moses. He loves us and will help us to love like Jesus!

Your Turn

What command did Jesus give to his friends?

How do you think that love is different from the "love your neighbor as yourself" kind?

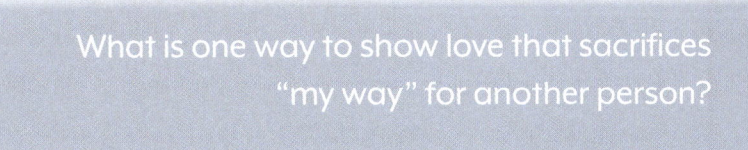

What is one way to show love that sacrifices "my way" for another person?

Week 11 • Day 5

LOVE Logos!

Besides thinking of ways to respond in love to people, let's have fun making some artistic LOVE logos! Take a little time to look at logos online or in magazines to get ideas. Then go for it!

What You'll Need

- poster board or heavy paper
- pencil and eraser
- colored markers or other art materials (paint, watercolor pencils, etc.)
- scissors
- ruler
- masking tape or sticky tack

What You'll Do

1. Look up logos online or in magazines with a parent's permission.

2. Sketch out some logo ideas on paper. Remember, these are just ideas so be creative!

3. Choose some of your sketch ideas and transfer them onto the poster board. Make your logos large enough to place on the wall of your room.

4. Use the art materials to decorate your logos.

5. Cut the logos out.

6. Use masking tape or sticky tack to attach them to the walls of your room.

Now, when you see your logos, you'll remember to love others the way Jesus loves you!

Prayer

Dear God, It sounds hard to love others the way Jesus loves us. But I'm drawing a way I want to love like that. Let my drawing be a prayer. Thank you that you make this kind of love possible through your Holy Spirit. In Jesus' name, amen.

Week 11 • Day 6

Love Your Neighbor

Showing that you love others doesn't need to be dramatic or expensive. You can show people that you love them by doing some of the following things:

1. Ask your parents to help you find someone who needs help with yardwork or housework. Have them set up a time when you will go with them to that person's house and do the work that needs to be done. Before you go, make a list together of the tools and items you'll need.

2. Bake goodies and serve your neighbors. Make enough cookies or cupcakes to share. Deliver them with your parents. If you don't know your neighbors well, take time to talk with them, too!

3. Have a party in your front yard and invite your neighbors. It can be simple: offer ice cream, cookies, and drinks. Set out lawn chairs so that people can talk with each other. You can play simple "get to know you" games such as lining up by birthday (not the year, but the month and day) or by the first letter of each person's first name.

Bonus: Love Bombs

Loving people can be frustrating—it can also be fun! Here's a simple way to show love and serve others with that sacrificial love Jesus talked about: we call them "LOVE BOMBS."

1. Choose a person you are going to love bomb. (Maybe start with your mom, just for practice!)

2. Write down one thing you love about that person. ("Your smile makes everyone else smile!" or "I see the way you are patient.")

3. For every day of that week, make a one- or two-sentence note. You don't have to sign your name unless you want to. These notes are not about you. They are notes to encourage the person you are love-bombing.

Find a way every day to secretly slip that note onto the person's desk, into their pocket, on the seat of the car—you get the idea. You're a stealth bomber of encouragement! You'll have fun and someone else will be blessed and encouraged!

Week 12 • Day 1

Confessing to God

If we confess our sins to him, he is faithful and just to forgive us our sins and to cleanse us from all wickedness.

1 JOHN 1:9

If you forgive those who sin against you, your heavenly Father will forgive you. But if you refuse to forgive others, your Father will not forgive your sins.

MATTHEW 6:14-15

Forgetting Who You Are

EXODUS 32:1-12,30-32; JOHN 8:1-11,16,24; ROMANS 5:8,18-19

Surprising Similarities

Interceding!

- Moses often **interceded** for the Israelites and begged God to forgive them. When the Israelites worshiped the golden calf at Mt. Sinai, Moses interceded twice for them. The second time, he even offered his own life in exchange for theirs.

> **Intercede**
> to stand in between two people or groups who are arguing

- Jesus interceded for us—he gave his own life in exchange for ours. Now, in Heaven, he intercedes for his people.

Confessing!

- Even though the Israelites were caught worshiping an **idol** (breaking the first and second commandments!) some of them would not confess their sin. They had to pay for their sin themselves with their lives.

> **Idol**
> an image of a god

- When Jesus was on earth, he met quite a few religious people who thought they were the "good people." They were not willing to confess their sin. Jesus told them that they, too, would die in their sins. If we want to be forgiven, we need to **confess**—tell the truth about what we have done.

> **Confess**
> To say what is true about a situation

Moses was up on the mountain with God for a very long time and the Israelites began to doubt God's power. The people asked Aaron, Moses' brother, to make them an idol. A few weeks before, they had told God that they would do everything God had said. But without Moses around, those things God had said didn't seem very important. Lots of trouble came to them because of this sin—and still, some of them would not confess that they had sinned!

Still, Moses interceded for the Israelites. And he was serious about it! *Read Exodus 32:30–32 to find out how serious Moses was about asking God to forgive them.* God forgave the Israelites for Moses' sake. He loved Moses and he loved them.

The Bigger Story

When Jesus lived on earth, he loved everyone. The religious leaders often wanted to prove that Jesus was not a good person because he threatened their authority. Besides that, he often told people, "Your sins are forgiven." That made the religious leaders very upset. "Only God can forgive sin," they would grumble. In their hearts they had to wonder, "So if only God can forgive sin, is this really the Messiah? God's Chosen One? Is that why he forgives sin?"

One time at the temple, Jesus was surrounded by a crowd of religious leaders. They dragged a woman to the center and forced her to stand right in front of Jesus. These leaders said the woman had been caught with another woman's husband. They reminded Jesus that law said she should be killed. *Read John 8:6 to find out why they asked Jesus what he thought.*

Jesus wasn't upset by their noise and their questions. He squatted down next to the woman and began to write in the dust. But the leaders wouldn't leave him alone. They kept on saying, "What do *you* say about this? You're the teacher!"

What did Jesus do? Read John 8:7–9 to find out! What do you think Jesus was writing in the dirt? Whatever it was, it made the men ashamed. It reminded them that they were sinners, too. But they wouldn't admit it. They left, one by one—until only Jesus was left. Jesus turned to the woman and asked her, "Where are those men? Has no one **condemned** you?"

The woman must have smiled a little bit. She said, "No one, sir."

Jesus said, "Then I don't condemn you either. Go now—and don't sin anymore."

She was forgiven by Jesus!

Condemn
to disapprove or blame

What's That Mean to Me?

God is holy. That means he cannot be where there is sin. But God loves everyone and that is why he sent Jesus. Jesus was willing to be punished for ALL the wrong of ALL the people so that we can be forgiven of ALL our sin! Forever! That's even greater than Moses being willing to die for his people. Jesus died for all our sin, so we all could come close to God.

God's Word says that if we will confess—tell the truth about what we have done—and ask God to forgive us, he will. He wants us to turn away from sin and be close to him.

Week 12 • Day 2

Your Turn

What did the Israelites learn about the importance of obeying God's commands?

What did Jesus do so that we can be forgiven?

What do you think happens if we refuse to confess our sins?

Prayer

Dear Jesus,

Thank you for taking the punishment for my sin, so that I can be holy in God's sight. Thank you that when I confess what I have done, you forgive my sin. I am thankful you made it possible to be forgiven. In Jesus' name, amen.

Week 12 • Day 3

Who I Am

One reason we sometimes fall into sin is that we forget who God says we are. Then, we listen to lies like, "I have to do it myself," or "people don't like me," or that "I'm not good enough"—things like that. Paul tells us that "If you do anything you believe is not right, you are sinning" (Romans 14:23). So today, find out "who God says I am." When we remember who God says we really are, it makes us strong in him! Look up each of these verses and match them to the words in the word box. (Note: One verse has four correct answers!)

God says I am . . .

1 Peter 2:9

Ephesians 5:1

Romans 4:7

1 Corinthians 6:17

Ephesians 6:10

Romans 15:7

> chosen
> royal priests
> holy nation
> God's possession
> God's children,
> accepted
> strong
> one in spirit

Answers on Page 221

Prayer

Dear God, I don't want to be separated from you. I do wrong. And others do wrong to me. I want to keep on forgiving and being forgiven. Please help me to come to you and get your help to forgive others. In Jesus' name, amen.

Week 12 • Day 4

What Is Forgiveness?

If we confess our sin, God is faithful to forgive us. *Read what Jesus said in Matthew 6:14–15 about forgiveness.* That is kind of a surprising thing Jesus said, right? Why do you think Jesus said this? Isn't it just "confess and be forgiven"?

Jesus is making it clear that the purpose of forgiveness is to be completely clean, with nothing between us and God. Sin is separation from God. Sin makes us turn away so that God won't see something we're holding onto. Think about a toddler who's got a cookie she wasn't supposed to have!

Jesus wants us to understand: Unforgiveness isn't just hurt feelings. It is sin.

"But wait!" you say. "Can't I hold a grudge if someone did something terrible to me? Isn't it OK to hang onto that? I mean, they really hurt me badly!" God says no. It's not enough to ask God to forgive some sin, but not ALL of it! When I ask God to forgive my sin but I won't forgive that other person, I'm choosing to hold onto sin. When I won't forgive the other person, then I shouldn't expect God to forgive me of my sin.

Now let's be clear about what forgiveness is NOT:

- Forgiveness is not a feeling; it is a choice.
- Forgiveness doesn't mean that what the other person did was OK.

- It doesn't mean trusting that person again.
- It is not pretending we were not hurt.
- It doesn't mean that the person is not responsible for what they did.
- It's not letting that person keep on hurting us.

Forgiveness is:
- Coming to God and telling him about the situation.
- Telling God how you feel.
- Asking God to show you what you need to know about the situation.
- Asking God to help you forgive.

The important thing is to take it to God and get his help, not be running off like that toddler with a cookie. There may be times when we think we have forgiven, but then something happens that shows us we haven't forgiven the other person completely.

It is like the layers of an onion. You think you have peeled away the last layer but then you see another layer. Don't be discouraged. Just keep on forgiving as God shows you more places you didn't forgive. Eventually, you will have no anger towards them and then you'll be free!

Your Turn

What are some things forgiveness does not mean?

Why does God want us to forgive others?

Once we have turned away (like that toddler with a stolen cookie), we have separated from God. How else would you describe sin? How do our actions show our being separated?

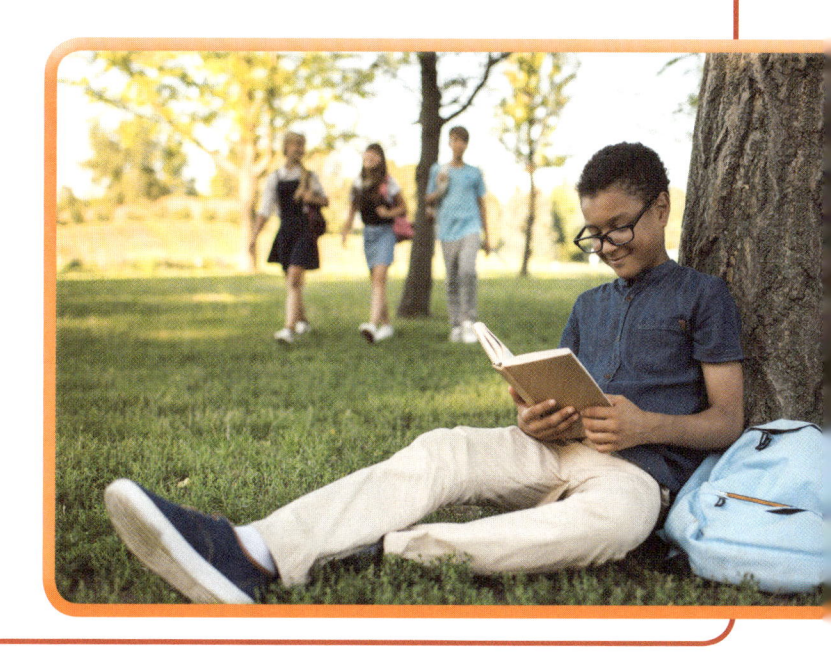

Week 12 • Day 5

Fresh Start Life Hacks

What do we do when we have a problem? We go to the internet and type in our question! Sometimes the advice is great. Sometimes it is worthless. But today, let's pretend we are life hack experts in helping people make a fresh start through forgiveness.

What You'll Do

You have some options with this activity. Either:

- Read these aloud to your family and get their ideas
- Write out a response to one or two of these life-hack questions

The goal is to answer the question: What would you say to each person?

Dear FSLHE (Fresh Start Life Hack Expert),

A kid at school always makes fun of me. I have never said anything back, but I really don't like her. I found out today that she was in a serious bike accident. I feel terrible! What do I do?

Ill Wisher

Dear FSLHE (Fresh Start Life Hack Expert),

I found some cans of spray paint that were left in the garage. I decided I should try them out, just for fun. I did a little art on a construction fence, so it wasn't a big deal. But the security guard caught me. He called the police! Now my parents are SOOOO mad. What can I do? I'm really in trouble.

Art Notter

Dear FSLHE (Fresh Start Life Hack Expert),

I saw a t-shirt at the store that I really liked—but it didn't have any money. I managed to stuff the shirt under my sweatshirt and walk out. When my parents asked about the shirt, I told them a kid at school didn't want it, so he gave it to me. Now I feel like God is mad at me. What can I do?

Tee Taker

Dear FSLHE (Fresh Start Life Hack Expert),

I'm so mad at Myra right now, I could beat her up! You wouldn't believe what she said about me. And she said it in front of the whole class. What she did is unforgivable. I'm NEVER going to forgive her for this. What do you say? Am I right, or am I right?

Furious Frieda

Week 12 • Day 6

En-Courage Mats

You don't have to do something wrong to need encouragement. Make an en-courage mat for yourself. Then make one for another family member to be bold in God.

What You'll Need

- 2 sheets of paper in different colors
- markers or crayons
- scissors
- tape
- **Optional:** clear Con-Tact paper

What You'll Do

1. On one sheet of colored paper, draw designs, and color it brightly.

2. On the other sheet of colored paper, write words that would help a person be bold in God. Use empowering Bible verses like 1 Timothy 4:8, 1 Corinthians 16:13, or Luke 1:45. Or, use phrases such as, "God will help you!" or "I can do everything through Jesus" or "Be bold in God."

3. Cut one sheet of paper into strips that are less than an inch (two fingers' width) wide.

4. Fold the other paper in half "hot dog" style—lengthwise. On the folded edge, cut slits about an inch (or two fingers' width) apart. Cuts can be wavy or crooked. They should be about three and a half inches long.

5. Open the folded paper. Keep each strip face up as you weave a strip over-and-under through your slits. Push it all the way to one side.

6. Next, weave a strip under-and-over through the slits. Keep going, over-and-under with the next strip, then under-and-over with the strip after that. Keep pushing the woven strips toward the side where you started.

7. Once you've woven all your strips through, use tape to hold the strips in place.

Optional: If you want your mat to last, lay clear Con-Tact paper over it. (Ask someone to help with this.)

Week 13 • Day 1

Sticking with God

God can be trusted to keep his promise.

HEBREWS 10:23

Jesus Christ is the same yesterday, today and forever.

HEBREWS 13:8

Promised Land

NUMBERS 13:1–14:38, DEUTERONOMY 31:1-8, PHILIPPIANS 2:6-8

Surprising Similarities

Twelve is the Number!

- Moses chose twelve men to go into the Promised Land and report on what they found.

- Jesus chose twelve disciples to go into the world to tell about the true Promised Land—God's Kingdom.

Ten and Two: Fearful or Faithful?

- Of the twelve men that Moses sent to spy out the land, ten were afraid. Only two believed God would keep his promise to give them the land. Those two, Caleb and Joshua, were the only people of their generation who entered the Promised Land.

- Of the twelve men Jesus chose to be his disciples, one betrayed him (Judas Iscariot) and one denied him (Peter). But after the Holy Spirit came, Peter became the first bold preacher of the good news of Jesus.

Through Jericho!

- Under Joshua's leadership, the Israelites entered the Promised Land through Jericho.

- Jesus went up through Jericho to Jerusalem to die on the cross.

The twelve men Moses sent out had seen the amazing things God's Promised Land had. They brought back samples of fruit, they told about the beautiful place, but ten of them were afraid that the people who already lived in the land would kill them. They told how big and scary these people were. Soon everyone was whining and wanting to go back to Egypt again.

Only Caleb and Joshua believed that if God had said they could take the land, then he would make that possible! God was so tired of the people not trusting him that he decided no adults who had left Egypt would go into the land. They would all die of old age, still traveling in the desert, except for Caleb and Joshua.

They say it takes about eleven days to walk from Egypt to Israel. But it took them FORTY YEARS of wandering around. When they crossed the Jordan River, they took the land, just as God said they would. But only Caleb and Joshua got to see that happen. Even Moses died before they entered the Promised Land.

The Bigger Story

How did Jesus show that he had full confidence in his Father God? Because he fully trusted God, he always obeyed God. *What kind of obedience did Jesus give? Read Philippians 2:6–8.* Jesus left all the privileges of heaven, became a servant of the lowest kind—and then, literally obeyed God his Father even though he knew he was going to die. *Why do you think Jesus was willing to do this? Read 2 Corinthians 5:17–18.* Jesus was willing to die because he loves you that much. He loves me that much. He trusted God his Father's faithfulness so much that he was willing to die and trust God to raise him back to life. That's a lot of trust! But Jesus rose to life again! He did this so that he could **reconcile** everything—to bring everything back to God!

> **Reconcile**
> to bring two people together, to make peace or restore friendship

What's That Mean to Me?

Jesus promised that he is preparing a place for us. *Read this promise in John 14:1–6.* Jesus said that we can be with him forever in Heaven and he is **faithful**.

How do we get to that place Jesus is preparing? Jesus said, "I AM the way!" Remember John 3:16? (You learned it in week 6!) When we believe in Jesus and ask to be part of God's family, he says we can be part of his Kingdom here and now, and then live with him forever in Heaven! That's even greater than living in the best place on earth!

> **Faithful**
> trustworthy, reliable, unchanging, promise-keeping

No matter how sad, bad or hard things look at times, God always keeps his promises. We can trust him whether things look great to us or whether they look awful. He sees farther than we can see. He knows what is coming. We are part of God's kingdom—and he is the king who can do anything!

Week 13 • Day 2

Your Turn

What did Jesus do to show he trusted God?

What does it mean that Jesus reconciled us to God?

What is a way you have seen God's faithfulness in your life or the life of someone you know?

Prayer

Dear God, I'm glad you are faithful. I'm drawing something that reminds me of what my life might look like if you were not faithful. Thank you! In Jesus' name, amen.

Week 13 • Day 3

Scout for Good

Moses sent twelve scouts to the Promised Land. Only two came back with good news. Today, you can scout for good, too.

What You'll Need

- latex or rubber gloves
- 2 or more trash bags

What You'll Do

1. As you walk, look around. What do you see?

2. Walk to wherever you see trash and pick up every piece you spot.

3. Fill one bag with trash. Fill the other bag with things that can be recycled: cans, bottles, paper, etc.

For more fun, do this with a friend. Each of you fills two bags. Who found the most trash? Who found the most recyclables?

Bonus Fun

- Put some felt inside a can to make a glasses holder.
- Build a terrarium with plastic soda bottles. Add some dirt and leaves. Then, add animals figurines.

You can do so much with recycled things!

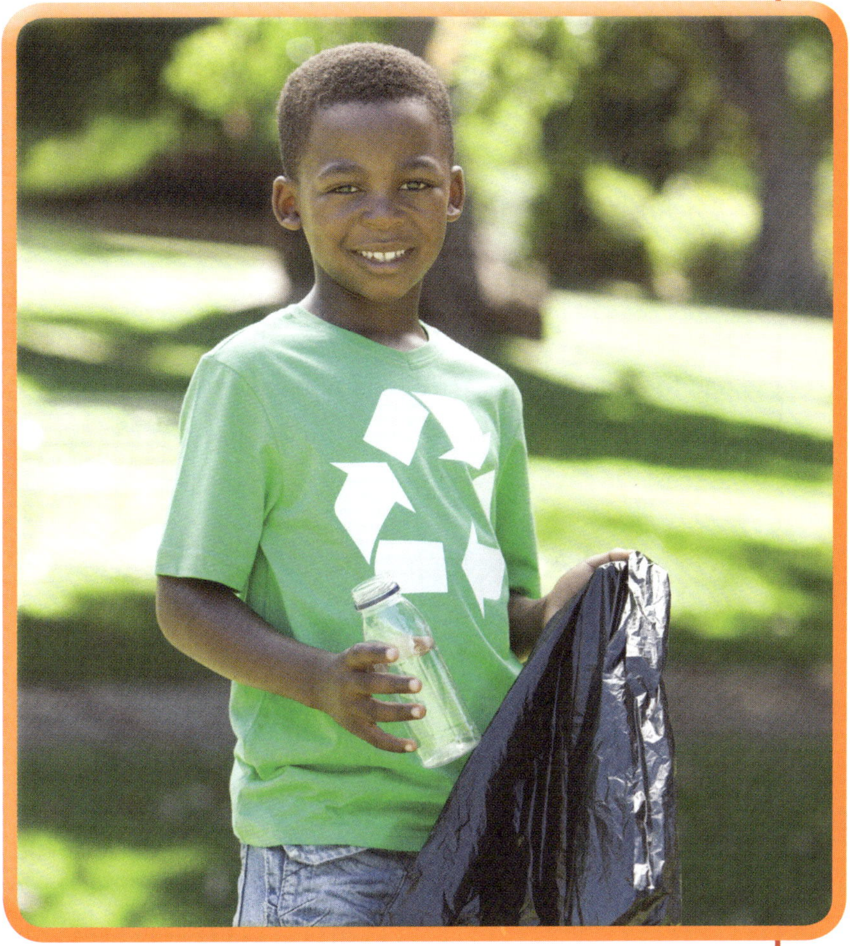

Week 13 • Day 4

Growing in Faithfulness

We've talked a lot about how God is faithful, trustworthy, promise-keeping, never-changing, and always-loving. He's proven over thousands of years that he is worthy of our complete trust! We've talked about how Caleb and Joshua were faithful—that is, they simply believed God when everyone else said "No! We can't do it!" That kind of believing is faithfulness, too—in the sense of being "faith-FULL" when everyone else is "faith-LESS"!

We've also talked about the way Jesus was so full of faith that he trusted God his Father even when it meant he had to die. And then trust God to bring him back to life. That is being full of faith! Jesus showed us what it's like to trust God when everything else screams, "No!"

Someone once said, "Faith is spelled 'r-i-s-k.'" That is because faith can be risky. Lots of times, we're told to "play it safe" like the Israelites did. Scared of the giants they had never seen, they would rather wander in the desert until they died. They were safe—God took care of them, fed them, protected them—but they never entered the land God promised. They never had the great adventure of obeying God because they never trusted him enough to do what he said! They were safe. And they missed the greatest joy of their lives.

That's where a lot of us end up. God's loving us, taking care of us, leading us, but instead of follow God on a faith adventure, we get "ten-spy-itis." It's the disease where we decide God's way is too risky. We sit down in our little desert and stay there, waiting for the manna. And we get fed. And our lives are so boring. And we wonder why it's not more exciting to follow Jesus. So we do other things we think are exciting, but those get boring, too. You see, we were made to trust God and follow Jesus on the great faith adventure. That's why those other things don't satisfy us!

Joining Jesus on the great faith adventure might scare you silly sometimes. But the thing to remember is that you can ALWAYS trust God to do what he says he will do! That's the reason we can be confident to obey him!

It's easy to be a "ten-spy-guy." No one will ever know except you, just what faith adventures you skipped because you were fearful instead of faith-full. But give it a try. Just once. You'll find that the adventure is so much fun, so satisfying, it's worth it!

R-I-S-K

Your Turn

What good, logical reasons did the ten spies have for not believing God? (See Numbers 13:27–33)

What reason did Caleb and Joshua have for believing God?

On a scale of 1–10, how faith-full was Jesus? On that same scale, how faith-full do you think you might be?

Week 13 • Day 5

Faithful Letters

People in the Bible wrote faithful letters to remind themselves of God's goodness when times were tough. Today, you get to write your own faith letter.

First, brainstorm names for God that describe his faithfulness—like shepherd, king, friend, guide, protector, miracle-worker—you get the idea. Fill in some of your ideas in your personal psalm! Use the space below to brainstorm before you write your answers on the next page.

I _____ to you, Lord, because you are _____.

You are like a _____ to me.

You give me _____ and you tell me _____.

You are like a _____ to me.

You show me _____ and you do this for me: _____.

I _____ for joy and I _____ before you, Lord!

You have made my heart _____.

You are like the best _____ anyone could ask for—only far, far better!

I give you my thanks. I give you my _____.
I give you all my _____, forever.
You are worthy of _____.

Week 13 • Day 6

Growing in Faithfulness

Today, we're going to celebrate God's faithfulness with a project that reminds us how much we have grown in faith-full-ness!

What You'll Need

- watercolor paper
- crayons
- fine-tip permanent marker
- watercolor paint
- paintbrushes

What You'll Do

1. On your paper, draw a small circle in the center in crayon.

2. Around it, draw concentric circles that look like tree rings. Draw a ring for each year of your life.

3. In the space between crayon lines, write (in marker) about times the Lord blessed you or your family. For example, in the first ring, which represents you as a one year old, how was your family blessed?

4. Now choose some watercolors you like. Use them to paint over your project in any way you think looks good. You can even blot off the watercolor and start again while it's still wet.

5. As you paint, thank God for the ways you just see that he has been faithful to you. Thank him for the ways you've learned to be faithful and faith-full! It's a beautiful reminder!

6. When the paper is dry, hang it on a wall— or even frame it. It will look great!

Prayer

Dear God, I admit it—sometimes I am scared about what other people will say. I'm afraid someone will make fun of me if I follow you on a faith adventure. But I want to learn to be faith-full, not faith-less. I'm drawing something to remind myself how I look to you when I am faith-full! Help me be like that! In Jesus' name, amen.

Answer Key

Pages 54-55, Zero to Hero

1. Albert Einstein
2. Thomas Edison
3. Joni Eareckson Tada
4. Ludwig van Beethoven

Pages 72-73, Power Words

Across

3. Strong
6. Force
7. Leader
8. Authority
9. God

Down

1. Miracle
2. Preach
4. Persuade
5. Control

Page 118, Bound or Free?

Everyone who sins is a slave to sin. . . . If the son sets you free, you will be free indeed.

Page 134, Godly Guiding

Jesus looked at them intently and said, "Humanly speaking, it is impossible. But not with God. Everything is possible with God." Mark 10:27

Pages 168-169, Wall of Words

It is impossible to please God without faith. Anyone who wants to come to him must believe that God exists and that he rewards those who sincerely seek him.

Page 194, Who I Am

1 Peter 2:9—royal priests, chosen, holy nation, God's possession

Ephesians 5:1—God's children

Romans 4:7—forgiven

1 Corinthians 6:17—one in spirit

Ephesians 6:10—strong

Romans 15:7—accepted

Moses and Jesus and Me!

Moses and Jesus and Me! brings cool devotionals to children ages 6-9 and 10-12. These devotionals from Gotta Have God devotionals for boys and God and Me! devotionals for girls are packed with insightful stories, meaningful prayers, awesome memory verses, and fun activities that will help boys and girls draw closer to God every day. Each devotional draws on the same Bible content, so boys and girls of different ages can learn the same biblical truths together.

222 pages each, Paperback, Full Color

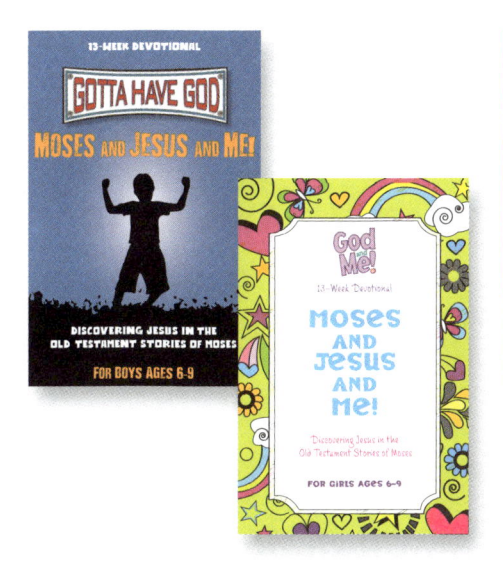

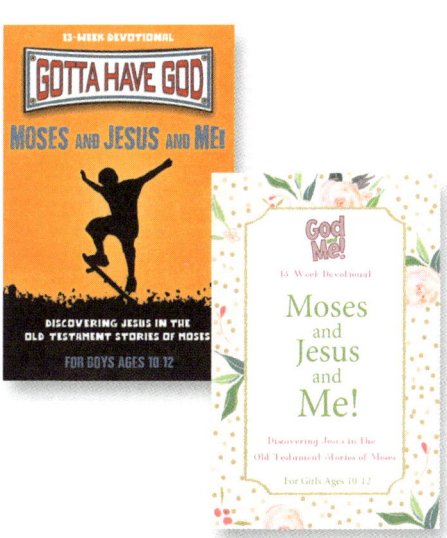

Moses and Jesus and Me! For Boys Ages 6–9	L50035	ISBN: 9781628628135
Moses and Jesus and Me! For Girls Ages 6–9	L50036	ISBN: 9781628628142
Moses and Jesus and Me! For Boys Ages 10–12	L50038	ISBN: 9781628628319
Moses and Jesus and Me! For Girls Ages 10–12	L50039	ISBN: 9781628628326

Find more great books by visiting **www.hendricksonrose.com/RoseKidz**.

SUPER INCREDIBLE FAITH SERIES FOR GIRLS AND BOYS

Help your children better understand how much God loves them! In these books, boys and girls will be encouraged to develop positive character traits and rely on God to help them in any circumstance.

***Living Bravely*, Ages 6 to 9.**
***Conquering Fear*, Ages 10 to 12**
320 pages, Paperback, Full Color Illustrations

| Living Bravely | L50020 | ISBN: 9781628627800 |
| Conquering Fear | L50021 | ISBN: 9781628627824 |

GUIDED JOURNALS FOR GIRLS AND BOYS

Preteen boys and girls will love these daily devotional journals that really encourage them to dig into the Bible. **Ages 10–12.**

136–160 pages, Paperback, Illustrated

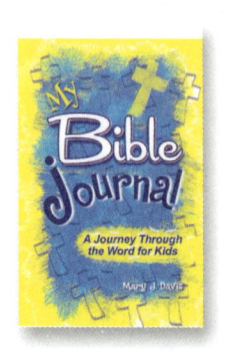

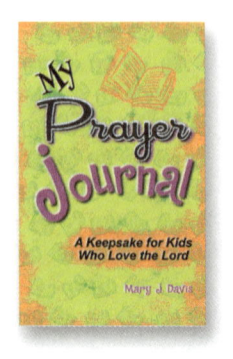

| My Bible Journal | L46911 | ISBN: 9781885358707 |
| My Prayer Journal | D46731 | ISBN: 9781885358370 |

Find more great books by visiting **www.hendricksonrose.com/RoseKidz.**